HIP
HOTELS

BEACH

HERBERT YPMA

HIP
HOTELS

BEACH

with 511 illustrations, 396 in color

Thames & Hudson

introduction

Barefoot in the sand. More than just a dream, it's practically a primal urge. Once in a while, are we not all gripped by a deeply felt desire to shed our clothes and our sophisticated lives, and to opt instead for the sunny, warm, seductive sensuality of strolling toe-deep in the powdery white sand of a beautiful beach wearing little more than a bathing suit and a smile? Of course we are.

But then the ugly monster of practicality elbows its way back into our easily dissuaded psyches. In our busy-busy modern lives, time is precious, and none so precious as our time off. Beach? Yes, but where and why? If your only desire is to acquire a suntan, then there are thousands of choices at your disposal, each more banal than the next. You'll return with some colour, but you will not have travelled.

So let's be clear. Is this a guidebook to the world's best beaches? No. I may have spent (some might say wasted) a fair part of my life as a beach bum, but I would hate to be lumbered with the task of rating a beach. I wouldn't know what criteria to apply. The powdery consistency of the sand? This is a book of beach destinations for real travellers. If you choose to spend a few days on a beach in Australia, for example, why not make it a uniquely Australian experience? This is the great empty continent, the only place like it on earth. The Bay of Fires Lodge is one destination that gives you exactly that: vast unpopulated spaces, plenty of wallabies, wombats and echidnas, and all the surf and sweeping crescents of sand your imagination can conjure. In India, the beaches provide quite different sensations: exotic, vibrant, teeming with life, and with more fishing boats than sun-bakers. The charm and colour of the Caribbean; the vivid culture of the Mexican *pueblo*; the mystical power of the breathtaking, cliff-hanging, whitewashed islands of the Aegean – these are only some examples of the visual and vernacular variety the planet has to offer. The global diversity of beach life can be spectacularly evocative.

But even the most splendid locations for beaching it are nothing without an equally inspiring place to stay. The hotel has to be part of the experience. Fortunately, across the globe, imagination, creativity and aesthetic daring have combined to produce places to stay that amplify the best qualities of their setting. *Hip Hotels Beach* is about giving you, the beachcomber, an opportunity to participate in a real travel adventure while you are toe-deep in the sand.

carlisle bay

It's hard to believe, but there was a time when Antigua's abundance of sandy beaches was anything but a blessing. While other Caribbean islands were protected by rocky inhospitable shores, Antigua's countless coves made it an easy target for marauding bands of the predatory and much-feared Carib Indians. Long before Columbus reached the Americas, the island of Antigua had been inhabited by peaceful agrarian tribes who had made their way here from South America via Trinidad. That was roughly 4,000 years ago, when the world's oceans were about 275 feet lower, making inter-island journeys that much easier.

I confess I knew nothing about Antigua's pre-Columbian history until I read a handbook on the subject at Carlisle Bay. Like many people, my knowledge of the West Indies started with the plantation era, the days of the so-called evil triangle of trade. Ships transported African slaves to the Caribbean to work the plantations, and returned to mother England laden with the sugar, tobacco, cotton, etc., produced by their backbreaking labour. They completed the triangle by heading back to the coasts of West Africa. The truth is, culturally and historically, these islands are far more intricate and old than we imagine. And

though they are evocatively grouped together as Caribbean, they are each as distinct in geography, topography and anthropology as the various nations of Europe.

You could say that Antigua is the Ireland of the Caribbean. It's a colourful place, both in terms of its houses, painted a rainbow of bright tints, and in terms of its people, who have a fun-loving, feisty nature. Antigua is also surprisingly green. Away from the beaches, the island is a verdant vision of rolling pastures and the odd craggy peak. With a population of just 66,000, the majority of whom live in and around the capital St John's, most of the island is sparsely inhabited. Tourism has only really reached Antigua's outer perimeter. And even then, there are still plenty of stretches that remain undeveloped. Unlike chic St Barths or cosmopolitan Barbados, Antigua is remarkably untouched by the massive tourism that the Caribbean generates.

The lush countryside, the colour, the warm disposition of the people – these might be what distinguish Antigua from other Caribbean islands, but for Gordon Campbell Gray, the very successful proprietor of London's One Aldwych, the decision to invest in Antigua was swayed by the special beauty of Carlisle Bay.

This natural harbour in the most remote corner of the island, defined by a fine crescent of sand, is straight out of an ideal Caribbean press release. Its emerald green, crystal-clear waters are surrounded by forested mountains and plenty of swaying palms, with a small village nearby that consists entirely of brightly painted wooden clapboard houses. There's even the perfect Caribbean church on the headland. Best of all, there are not, nor ever will be, any other hotels to share it with. Campbell Gray's Carlisle Bay is the only hotel in this idyllic location and, having negotiated title to the entire beach, he intends to keep it that way.

Even before the two hundred-plus crew started building, the travel world was buzzing with anticipation. Why would such an urban and urbane operator venture to such a remote spot? What could he possibly offer that wasn't already available from the thousands of hotels that already exist in the Caribbean? The answer is a level of luxury and an attention to detail that may be the norm for the world's biggest cities, but is still quite novel in the Caribbean. From the specially selected lights that illuminate the garden at night, to the bleached grey stain of the outdoor timber, to the flowers (orchids, orchids and more orchids), to the custom-made furniture and interiors designed by London-based Mary Fox Linton – no detail large or small has escaped Gordon's magnificent obsession. The swimming pool tiles were brought in from Bali, a black-painted orchid pool defines the entrance, and the shop displays Vilebrequin swimwear. With the proprietor's assured taste, Carlisle Bay has been groomed as a Caribbean option for discerning adults.

The all-suites hotel opened in late 2003, and only time will tell if it can live up to all the pre-launch hype. But one thing is for sure: the guest reaps the benefit of Gordon Campbell Gray's almost manic attention to detail. It's a sexy combination: an ensemble of thoroughly tamed, perfectly trained, preternaturally well turned-out details – in a wild, undomesticated and ruggedly natural setting.

address   Carlisle Bay, Old Road, St Mary's, Antigua, West Indies

t +1 268 484 0000   **f** +1 268 484 0001   **e** info@carlisle-bay.com

room rates   suites from US$595

bay of fires lodge

I had a friend who moved to Melbourne from France. Every weekend he'd jump into his Rangerover and drive. 'Where do you go?' I once asked him. 'Nowhere in particular,' he replied. 'I just pick a direction and keep driving.' 'But why?' 'Because,' he explained, with almost childlike enthusiasm, 'I can drive for hours, sometimes days, without seeing a single person or any sign of civilization – no buildings, no road signs, no power lines, no telegraph poles.' He just couldn't get enough of the emptiness of this continent.

Going to the beach in Oz is not so different. Here you really can achieve the ultimate – a beach entirely to yourself, maybe even several. This vast island, a continent unto itself, is one of the few places in the world where such extravagant solitude is still possible. The Bay of Fires is on the far northeastern tip of Tasmania, on the edge of Mount William National Park. A magnificent succession of fine, white, crescent-shaped beaches interrupted by rounded granite headlands coloured bright red by lichens, this is an area of potent natural theatre: the reddest rock, the bluest water and the whitest sand, framed by rolling hills and densely verdant shrub. It is home to all sorts of indigenous fauna: wallabies, echidnas, brush-tail possums, wombats and Tasmanian devils, to name but a few. And the only building in this almost untouched coastal wilderness is the Bay of Fires Lodge. From a distance you would be hard-pressed even to spot it. Designed by Sydney architect Ken Latona, it's a thoroughly modern, almost transparent pavilion that respects Glen Murcutt's dictum that buildings should 'touch the earth lightly'. Scarcely a boulder or rock was disturbed in erecting this long wood and glass box that juts out of the surrounding bush like a spear to claim a sweeping view of the coast's extraordinary beaches.

The lodge's discreetly hidden structure houses ten double guest rooms, a library, a loft-style glass-sided dining room that seats twenty-four, a living room complete with an enormous contemporary cast-iron fireplace, a huge deck that doubles as an outdoor breakfast area, and another deck surrounded by bush. Electricity is solar-generated, the dunnies are organic compost toilets (which don't smell – not even a tiny bit), and the stainless steel showers are powered by pressure you provide by putting some old-fashioned elbow grease into a handpump beforehand. That said, the lodge has none of the woollen socks and sandals atmosphere often associated with 'green' places.

It's no crime to be a city-based capitalist here; just don't chuck your ciggy in the organic dunny.

One guest summed up the place with characteristic Australian understatement: 'Pretty good lodge, mate,' he volunteered in a distinctly Queensland twang. 'Would have been fun and games building this in the middle of nowhere.' So it was. Most of the materials were flown in by helicopter. The only road is a muddy, sandy goat path strictly limited to four-wheel-drive vehicles, and then only when the weather is reasonably dry. But that's the whole point of the Bay of Fires Lodge. It is meant to be inaccessible. All guests arrive on foot, complete with backpack and hiking boots. The lodge is the culmination of the second day of a guided walk that starts at a spot called Boulder Point and passes along the deserted beaches of Stumpy's Bay, Cobler Rocks, Cod Bay, Purdon Bay, Picnic Rocks, Deep Creek, Eddyston Point, Shell Coves, and finally to Abbotsbury Peninsula, location of the Bay of Fires Lodge. The first night is spent at a camp on Forester Beach, where your local guides prepare dinner using fresh local produce and seafood. You reach the Lodge at the end of the second day's trek; day three is spent sea-kayaking across nearby Ansons Bay. Midway through day four, guests depart on foot with their packs.

This is one hotel where the question 'What do you do there?' is totally redundant. But just as importantly, the Bay of Fires Lodge is no boot camp. It's what the most individual hotels in the world all are: an experience you will remember forever. For four days you don't just have a beach to yourself, you have an entire national park. (Well almost, but excursion groups are never bigger than ten.) And you stay in a place that effortlessly and stylishly combines the most compelling qualities of this extraordinary continent, namely virgin nature, stylish modern architecture and sophisticated new-style Mediterranean food – and of course those easy-going Aussies, who think it's the most natural thing in the world to be on a beach all by yourself.

address c/o 'Pleasant Banks', 170 Leighlands Rd, Evandale, P.O. Box 1879, Launceston, Tasmania 7250, Australia

t +61 (0)3 6391 9339 **f** +61 (0)3 6391 9338 **e** bookings@cradlehuts.com.au

rates from AU$1495 for all-inclusive four-day walk

ravesi's

Bondi Beach: the best-known crescent-shaped strand in the country. As an icon of the nation, Bondi is in the same league as the opera house and Ayers Rock. Yet when I first knew it, Bondi wasn't 'much cop', as they say in Australia. It had had its heyday. Prior to World War II it was Sydney's premier beach – site of the surf-lifesaving championships, an event that was the spirit of the nation incarnate. Braving the surf in an open lifeboat in the morning; tea with scones, clotted cream and cucumber sandwiches in the afternoon – it was the perfect mix of rugged, no-nonsense sportiness and English colonialism. Directly behind the beach in those days was a handsome pavilion where formal balls and tea dances were held, and just behind that was a two-lane boulevard divided by a majestic row of Norfolk pines.

After the war the pines died, the tea dances stopped, and surf-lifesaving was superseded by surfing, a completely individual sport that spurned all pomp and circumstance. All of a sudden Bondi was no longer Sydney's most desirable beach. That crown was stolen by the Northern Beaches – Manly, Dee Why, Avalon, Whale Beach and Palm Beach, to name but a few. Bondi was colonized by fish and chip shops, cheap accommodation, and RSL clubs –

venues for the Returned Servicemen's League, one third cheap casino, one third high-turnover bar and one third ballroom dancing. The art deco architecture that had once made the beach so fashionable was crumbling, but no one paid much attention. Bondi's only asset was simply that it was so close to Sydney's eastern suburbs, and not more than fifteen minutes from the heart of town. You could catch a few waves before work and still be in the office by nine. Its slightly sleazy image wasn't helped by the fact that the water was often murky. The city's main sewerage outlets were just offshore, and when the current and the prevailing wind were unfavourable, the swell was far from the clear blue idyl one would imagine of Australia.

The turning point came with a couple of extra miles of pipework. City sanitation extended the outflow further out to sea and instigated tertiary treatment. Within a few years Bondi's water sparkled again; in winter the dolphins returned, as did the odd whale. All of a sudden everyone started to see the potential of those art deco buildings, of the proximity to the city, of Bondi's elegant past, and that it still had pretty decent surf. In the past decade real estate prices have gone through the roof. But this is not a boom fuelled by investors.

Despite Bondi's trendiness, it still delivers the basics – white sand, blue sky and crystal-clear sea

Recently remodelled, the calm, cool, cocoa-coloured bedrooms are the perfect contrast to Ravesi's surfside location

Bondi's collection of candy-coloured art deco buildings makes it the South Beach of the southern hemisphere

Chocolate brown and white and the odd organic curve make up Ravesi's distinctly urban design signature

Big breakfast, big surf. Bondi Beach is less than fifteen minutes from the heart of Sydney, but still a great place to surf

Calm and restraint are key ingredients in Ravesi's appeal – the bar downstairs may be hopping, but your room won't be

It's driven by residents – people who want to live near the surf and enjoy an urban lifestyle at the same time. Bondi now has more restaurants, bars, cafés and brasseries than any other place in Sydney, perhaps all of Australia. Thai, Indian, Vietnamese, Turkish, Lebanese, Chinese – it's all available not more than a block from the beach, served in surroundings that take the design awakening in Oz very seriously.

In many ways Bondi is to Sydney what South Beach is to Miami – an enduring magnet for young, beachbound hipsters. Strangely enough, given its stellar reading on the hip scale, it's taken some time for Bondi to have a hotel that's up to the standards of the local restaurants, bars and cafés. The first and still the only one to break the mould is Ravesi's, right on the esplanade. This corner building used to be a rather tired apartment block, but there's hardly a trace of that today. Ravesi's glass and stainless steel bar opens out to the beach scene outside. Upstairs is an acclaimed restaurant and the rest is taken up by the newly renovated guest rooms. These are remarkably sober, perhaps as a response to all the colour, pattern and ethnicity of the surf scene. Everything is in shades of white, brown and grey. It sounds a bit strict but judging by the crowd in the bar and the queues for the restaurant, it's exactly the urbane thing to catch the boardies and thongs crowd.

For overseas visitors, Ravesi's is perfect. Like the Delano or the Shore Club in Miami, you don't have to go far to be in the thick of things – one or two floors down in the elevator to be exact. And there you are on a broad, mile-long crescent of fine sand with a surf that's perfect for long boards – they call them 'mini-Mals' (short for mini-Malibus) – in the middle, and shorter boards to the south. And that's the interesting twist: Bondi's renaissance has also seen surfing come in from the fringe. Mums, dads and kids surf together, grabbing their mini-Mals to catch a few waves before breakfast. Surf, sun and sand – it's the Sydney way.

---

address Ravesi's, 118 Campbell Parade, Bondi Beach, Sydney, NSW 2026, Australia

t +61 (0)2 9365 4422 **f** +61 (0)2 9365 1481 **e** ravesis@bigpond.com.au

room rates from AU$125

the landing

Harbour Island is everything the Bahamas should be and mostly aren't. The Caribbean dream is straightforward: hibiscus and palm trees and beautiful timber houses painted in bright gelato colours, with whitewashed picket fences. Plus of course crystal-clear turquoise waters lapping at the edges of exquisitely deserted beaches. The reality, particularly in Nassau, is (mostly) vastly different. There are endless duty-free tourist emporiums, and more than enough cruise ship passengers on day leave to make them viable. Hotels come in three sizes: large, very large, and way too large. The few cute little houses to survive are forlorn and distinctly out of place.

Then there is Harbour Island. Take a plane from Miami to Eleuthera, a taxi to the local wharf and a small speedboat across the bay and you've arrived at the Bahamian version of Capri – minus the crowds. This island is too remote for daytrippers (minimum two hours by fast ferry from Nassau) and the waters are too shallow for cruise ships. And unlike Mustique, another perfect little Caribbean island, Harbour Island is not exclusively given over to vacation homes for the rich and famous. There's a genuine local culture here which brings together expat residents with indigenous Bahamians. The result is something real – not too perfect and not too rustic. The other beauty of Harbour Island is the scale: small wooden houses, some dating back two centuries; small roads, mostly covered in sand; small buildings – no high-rise hotels, no apartment blocks, no condominiums, nothing in fact above two stories high. The whole place is just pink-sand beaches and brightly painted clapboard houses.

When the British first arrived here in the 1700s, they quarried the local coral-stone and used it to build stately houses with wooden verandahs. One such property, one of the most important on the island, is now a hotel called the Landing – because it's literally a stone's throw from the dock where the mailboats and water taxis arrive. It's the perfect Caribbean island guesthouse. With a cool interior of chalk-white walls, mahogany-stained wooden floors and immaculate white linen draped on massive four-poster beds and Chippendale chairs, the style is exactly right, a crisp patrician look with a distinctive British colonial signature.

Places like this always have a special story, and the Landing is no exception. It started with a blind date – a blind date that went wrong.

29

Harbour Island is just the way we like to imagine the Caribbean – colourful, charming and unspoilt

Quirky, effortless, authentic – there's no style formula at work here, just simple good taste

A stone's throw from the main jetty, the hotel is housed in one of the island's earliest colonial buildings

The decor of the Landing never feels 'decorated'; it is casually elegant and convincingly timeless

The restaurant is a real drawcard, with its sophisticated wine list and a world-class chef from Sydney

Designers David Flint Wood and India Hicks fused carefree Caribbean culture with British colonial form and formality

Toby Tyler was a bachelor living the good life in Sydney when friends called to invite him to dinner, hoping to matchmake him with their visitor, a model from New York. Not only was it not love at first sight, but they didn't even particularly like each other. But because of mutual friends they kept meeting, and by the time Tracy Barry – originally from the Bahamas, and the daughter of a former Miss Bahamas – was ready to leave, they were making plans to get married and settle in Sydney. But first Tracy had some loose ends to tie up, which included making some decisions about a family property on Harbour Island, a grand old house that had been run as a hotel – not very successfully. They made the decision to sell the place, and Toby accompanied Tracy to help organize things.

What happened next no doubt happens to a lot of people who come to Harbour Island… they couldn't bear to leave. Toby, a veteran of the catering business in Sydney, convinced Tracy to hold the sale until he had had a look at the books. He was convinced the answer lay in opening a top-class restaurant that would lure future guests, but also help tide them over out of season. He managed to convince one of Sydney's top chefs, Ken Gomes, to move to Harbour Island and he and his new wife set about a massive top-to-toe renovation.

Food aside, the Landing's greatest quality is aesthetic integrity. It feels like old money lightened up and toned down by its laid-back location. The look is a result of collaboration with locals David Flint Wood and India Hicks, whose own hilltop home has featured in just about every interiors magazine worldwide. She is the daughter of the late David Hicks and although she made her name modelling, the design gene eventually reasserted itself. Harbour Island being the place it is, it's no surprise they all ended up working together on the Landing. David and India did the design, Toby created the restaurant, and Tracy runs the place. The result is straight out of a Hemingway story, a relaxed, barefoot destination where life revolves around drinks at six and dinner at eight.

---

address The Landing, P.O. Box 190, Harbour Island, Bahamas

t +1 242 333 2707 **f** +1 242 333 2650 **e** info@harbourislandlanding.com

room rates from US$190

the house

Right now the Caribbean is hot. And I'm not talking about the weather. The handbrake is still firmly on long-haul travel since September 11, and there's extra uncertainty caused by the SARS scare in Asia. Now there's bird flu to worry about, plus the increasing avalanche danger that is marring the traditional winter vacations in the Alps, a direct result of seesawing winter temperatures. All in all, the aqua green waters and sparkling white beaches of these islands that Columbus first stumbled upon half a millennium ago seem the perfect antidote to the world's travel blues. And that doesn't look like changing any time soon.

The Caribbean in general, and Barbados in particular, seem to be immune to the goings-on in the wider world. The waters are still crystal clear, the beaches are straight off the cover of a travel brochure, the people smile a lot and the weather is almost always perfect. That's not to say that the island hasn't changed. Half a century ago Barbados was an upper-crust retreat, a venue for British aristocrats with triple-barrelled names and monogrammed steamer trunks. It was White Mischief with sand – on the beach instead of the plantation. They built beautiful homes on the tranquil west coast of the island, and entertained royalty, film stars, business titans and world leaders in equal shares. Today the colonial lifestyle is a thing of the past. All that remains of those days is some of the architecture and the location. While it's true that Barbados's Atlantic-facing east coast, the one even locals refer to as the Wild Coast, is increasingly being discovered by surfers and other adventurers, the west coast is still the thriving heartland of the island's tourism. But it's certainly no longer the preserve of the British elite. There are direct daily flights from London, while for New Yorkers the trip takes less than five hours. Barbados's sea, sand and sun are within easy reach these days, and are especially appealing at those times of year when back home you are more likely to find yourself holding a snow shovel than a vodka and tonic.

Yet for all its easy-going Caribbean-ness Barbados is one of the first islands in the region to have understood, astutely, that for many of these urban voyagers, sea, sand and sun are not enough. They also want to sample different restaurants and do a bit of shopping. In other words they want to do what they do in New York and London – with more skin on show. Like the British toffs who preceded them, the new Barbados crowd are not really inclined to

scale down their urban lifestyle – a lifestyle that the House was set up to serve.

Located just down the beach from Heron Bay and Sandy Lane – the institutions that kickstarted Barbadian tourism – the House is the beachside version of a hip downtown hotel. It's a scene on the sand. Populated by attractive young couples who are way too cool to be on honeymoon, the House is the venue for an extremely laid-back ritual that alternates between eating in the bar, swimming, sitting in the sun, drinking in the bar, swimming, sitting in the sun…until it gets dark, when the city gene reasserts itself and these chilled-out, suntanned, dressed-down urbanites revert to their primal role of restaurant stalkers. For this the House itself may be one of the best hunting grounds on the island, because the newest, most acclaimed, most *chichi* addition to the Barbados restaurant scene is the hotel's own Daphne's. Located bang on the beach, this satellite of the famous London restaurant is regarded by many as better than the original.

On a design front, its combination of ornate Persian-style floor-to-ceiling metal screens with teak furniture and floors is suitably exotic. Yet it's a beautifully intimate place with plenty of privacy for romantic dining. Its cuisine is also startlingly sophisticated, not least when compared with Barbadian classics like fried flying fish on a hamburger bun. Daphne's serves a metropolitan version of Italian dishes, with an emphasis on seafood. But good as it is, you are not bound to eat at Daphne's every night. From the House you can stroll along the beach to Lonestar, another acclaimed urban-style restaurant, or the Tides, or Josef's, or Fishpot, or La Mer, or Mango's by the Sea…. You get the idea.

Back at the hotel, it's interesting to note that the proprietors chose the name to suggest the ambience of renting a villa as opposed to staying in a hotel. They have a point. There are no brass buttons or reception desk in sight, and most guests seem quite happy to share the chef who came with the house.

address   The House, Paynes Bay, St James, Barbados, West Indies

t +1 246 432 5525   **f** +1 246 432 5255   **e** thehouse@eleganthotels.com.bb

room rates   from US$550

sandy lane

Sandy Lane is to Barbados what the Peninsula is to Hong Kong — except it's on the beach. They are both unashamedly luxurious. No feature, no facility, no detail has not been considered for the complete pampering of the guest. In any country Sandy Lane would be quite an achievement. In the sleepy, laid-back Caribbean, it's almost a miracle. The place is a well-oiled machine that seems to operate without hiccup or glitch. That said, I have to confess I was reluctant to investigate. I'm usually rather put off by grand hotels: too many people, too many staff fussing over you…and they have their own golf course.

But forget the golfers stuffed into their khaki shorts and polo shirts, with twenty years' of business lunches preceding them. Instead focus on the many many ways you can allow yourself to be spoilt. Because for the true hedonist, Sandy Lane is very hip indeed. People who know the place will tell you it always has been. It all started with Ronald Tree, a member of Winston Churchill's cabinet during World War II. He was in Trinidad on government business visiting Sir Edward Cunard (of Cunard shipping fame), then *aide de camp* to the governor of Trinidad. Tree mentioned to Cunard that he was considering buying a piece of real estate on Trinidad, and Cunard suggested perhaps he should take a look at Barbados instead, inviting him to stay in his own Barbadian home, Glitter Bay. It didn't take Tree long to fall in love with the island. Within a year he had purchased a chunk of land just down the coast from Glitter Bay. There he built Heron Bay, one of the most famous and theatrical houses in Barbados.

Heron Bay was designed in the uniquely Barbadian 'Caribbean Georgian' style. It is a classically proportioned Palladian mansion built entirely using coral-stone and coral mortar. This idiosyncratic but handsome construction method had been prevalent on the island since the booming heyday of the sugar industry and its thriving plantations. But as a building technique it developed largely out of necessity. In the early days of the plantations (1600–1750), timber was in ready supply, and as one English visitor noted in his book *A True and Exact History of the Island of Barbadous* (1657), 'the planters never consider which way they build their houses as long as they get them up.' In time, however, as wealth accumulated, matters of taste began to enter the equation, as did the more sober fact that the first wave of plantation building had cleared most of the island's trees.

Sandy Lane is distinguished inside and out by the soft, pale patina of its render, a paste of crushed coral limestone

Barbados's distinct 'Caribbean Georgian' style evolved during the heyday of the sugar plantations

After the first plantations cleared most of the island's trees, coral limestone became the chief building material

Sandy Lane is the perfect name for a hotel built directly adjacent to a long stretch of white sand and turquoise sea

While rebuilding Sandy Lane from scratch, the new owners preserved many details of its historic legacy

The Monkey Bar is entertaining and also appropriate, for Barbados still has a population of wild monkeys

But Barbados is built, rather conveniently as it turned out, on a cap of coral limestone. Colonial builders turned to this coral stone as a construction material. It was soft enough to be sawn by hand, and instead of paint or plaster the final structure could be coated with a thick paste mixed from quicklime and coral dust.

Ronald Tree entertained a host of royals, aristocrats and celebrities at Heron Bay. Within ten years word had spread about this idyllic stretch of Barbados's tranquil west coast, to the point that he began to envisage its potential as a tourist destination. Thus Tree purchased the Sandy Lane sugar estate just down the road and built a hotel in a similar style to Heron Bay on its 300-yard beach front. Opening in 1961, it was a success from the very start. With Tree's connections Sandy Lane quickly evolved into a luxury alternative to Jamaica's Round Hill.

So it may come as a surprise to hear that the Sandy Lane of today contains nothing of the original hotel. Acquired by new owners in 1998, the decision was made to demolish and rebuild the entire property from scratch in order to provide the services and facilities that modern standards of luxury demand. Yet in doing so, they adhered strictly to the aesthetic and techniques of the historic Caribbean Georgian style. It is a style that is more romanticized than ever today. Oliver Messel, the legendary set designer and celebrated island architect who designed many of the original villas on Mustique (including the late Princess Margaret's), did his finest work in Barbados, and chose to live here himself in the twilight of his life. None of this history and tradition was lost on the new proprietors of Sandy Lane, and in rebuilding the famous hotel the porches, the staircases, the walls, the symmetry, the columns and the glittering, creamy coral-stone construction – every characteristic Caribbean Georgian detail – were carefully adhered to. The end result is a thoroughly modern hotel on the inside that looks like it hasn't been touched on the outside.

address Sandy Lane, St James, Barbados, West Indies

t +1 246 444 2000 **f** +1 246 444 2222 **e** mail@sandylane.com

room rates from US$700

hi

The only thing missing is the letter 'P'. For such a Highly Individual Place, I just didn't get the name. Hi as in Hello? Hi as in the Doors song? But as I got acquainted with Hotel Hi, the answer became plain: they mean hi as in hi-tech.

It's not easy creating something genuinely new, but Hi succeeds in being different in every way. From the outdoor furniture to the food, the lighting, the bathrooms, the taps, the pool, the bar – the list goes on and on. There's a commitment to this project that reaches deep into every detail. As Mies van der Rohe used to say, there are no great designers, only great clients, and hiring Matali Crasset was a masterstroke on the part of the proprietors of Hi. A former protégée of Philippe Starck, Crasset is an industrial designer by training, which explains a great deal. More concerned with function and experimentation than with decoration, she is totally committed to the role of technology in design. With this project she got the chance to work in every design discipline that exists, including furniture, graphics, interiors and architecture.

There are nine different room concepts in this 38-room hotel, and with each new concept everything changes – and I mean everything.

Take the Indoor Terrasse rooms for instance. At first glance they look like open lofts. In the middle is a wooden platform with a mattress, some outdoor chairs and a swivelling flatscreen TV. The design concept is a take on an outdoor deck – indoors. At one end is a glass wall that screens the shower space and it in turn is camouflaged by a curtain of green, a row of lush palms in a box. To finish the fantasy, the toilet is in a little timber house in the corner, like a garden shed. Everything is controlled from a built-in panel of electronic buttons, including sliding steel shutters and the TV. It's a distinctly contemporary version of the sunken living room, executed with something Crasset obviously developed during her time with Philippe Starck – a sense of humour.

The rooms are divided into three price categories. The Indoor Terrasse and the equally inventive Happy Day occupy the medium price bracket, and the White & White duplex suites with spiral staircase leading to a private roof terrace are at the top end. Every shape, every material has been explored. Take for example something as ordinary as a sink: some are glass, some wood, some are in the shape of a black cone, some are marble rectangles. Leather, plastic, aluminium, wool, nylon – name it and

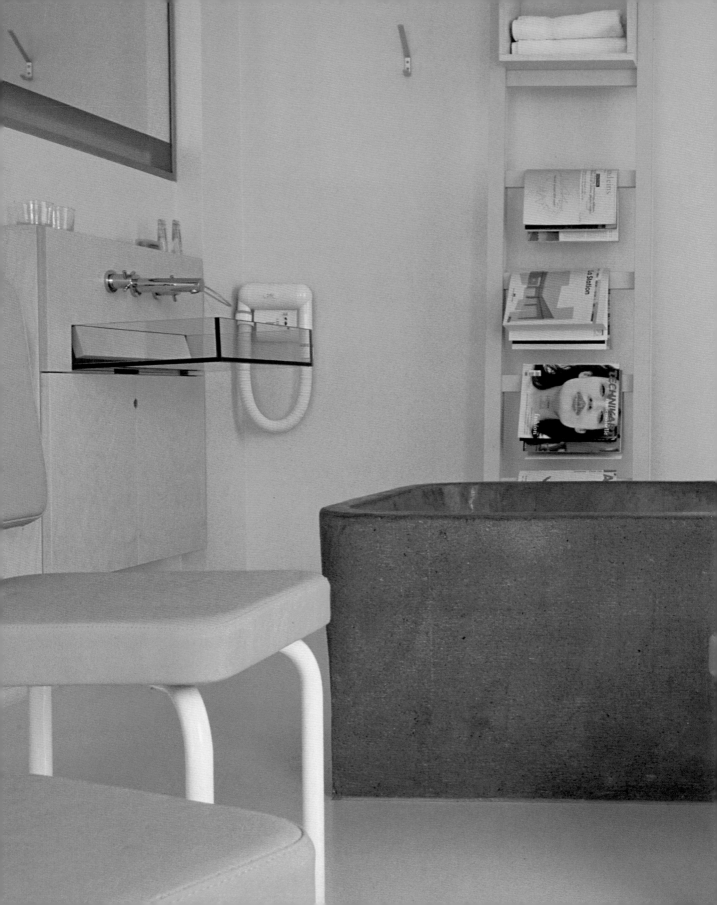

Crasset has used it as a design element. There's an inverted orange trapezoid-shaped pool on the roof, pink and purple internet stations in the lobby, and for those who like it bright, there are yellow executive suites on the top floor complete with solid black lava-stone bath in the middle of the room. And each of these is just one special design detail out of thousands.

Even eating and drinking were given the Matali treatment. Not only is the food multi-cultural (vermicelli à la Thai, *poulet* Tandoori, or chorizo and chickpea), but the presentation and delivery are straight out of a Luc Besson sci-fi film. A hi-tech pantry arranged in laboratory style along a corridor leads to the bar and restaurant. Everything is displayed in sealed glass jars, and that's also how it's brought to the table – on a lime green plastic tray also designed by Crasset (of course). Ordering the vermicelli on my first night, I couldn't understand why it was taking so long, until one of the staff politely pointed out that it had already been on the table for half an hour.

Stylistically, this place gets ten points for consistency, ten points for originality, and ten points for sheer commercial daring. Crasset's unique vision defines every detail and defies every convention. My favourite experience of all was breakfast. You grab a lime green tray and proceed to the pantry stocked with an incredible array of mini plates that bear everything from a range of hams to baby *chèvres*. But the real stars of the show are the stainless steel machines, one that squeezes orange juice – but only after the oranges have rolled down a stainless steel track – the other a self-service coffee machine the size of a small car that delivers the perfect cappuccino at the touch of a button.

But, you may ask, what kind of beach hotel is this? Where is the beach? Hotel Hi is an urban beach destination; the beach is a block away. For people who want to mix sea, sand and sun with cocktails, dinner and clubbing, Nice is rapidly emerging as the Miami of France.

---

address   Hotel Hi, 3 avenue des Fleurs, 06000 Nice, France

t +33 (0)4 97 07 26 26   **f** +33 (0)4 97 07 26 27   **e** hi@hi-hotel.net

room rates from €180

le manoir

One of the things Edith Wharton loved most about her château high above Hyères was the view she had of the islands just off the coast, the trio of silver slivers shimmering in the sea that are known as les Iles d'Or. And if she ever visited the most perfectly untouched of these islands, Port-Cros, I wonder if she would have cared to tell her friends about it – especially if she had had the pleasure to stay at Le Manoir.

This is one of those places that you will hesitate to tell anyone about – such a rare gem it seems almost obscene to share it. At the same time it's so special that the temptation to talk about it is irresistible. It's hard to put in words what makes Port-Cros and Le Manoir so special, but one that comes to mind is unspoilt. And that, in the South of France, is no easy condition to maintain. This stretch of coast is not only conveniently accessible (with two major airports and a TGV rail link), but what half a century ago was a collection of fishing villages is now home to millions of people. With ever easier access comes ever more tourism, and with millions of residents come shopping centres and franchises. In between all the American-style malls and the mushrooming apartment blocks, you're lucky to find even the odd beach or village. So the dream of having an idyllic island virtually to yourself seems not just improbable but almost insane.

Porquerolles, neighbour to Port-Cros, is quiet and relatively undeveloped. But it is a teeming metropolis compared to Port-Cros. All of this tiny island, including a maritime zone that extends a third of a mile around the coast, is a national park. Its only village consists of just seven buildings, three of them cafés. Le Manoir is its only hotel. A five-minute walk from the port, it is a whitewashed, green-shuttered, turreted affair straight out of a 1920s Lartigue photo of the Riviera. In a novel it would be the house of a wild but stylish aunt who escaped long ago, scandalously, with her lover to her own island, inherited from an eccentric but rich grandfather…and the funny thing is, this is not so far from the truth. For more than forty years Port-Cros was the private domain of Marcel Henry, a wealthy nobleman who fled the Riviera in 1920. Le Manoir was his retreat, and it was quite a love shack even before it became a hotel. His wife had become smitten with a tubercular poet, and she escaped to Port-Cros to be with her lover. Monsieur Henry purchased the island in an effort to win her back. In the end, husband, wife and suffering poet lived here together.

Le Manoir is still owned by a descendant of Marcel Henry, Pierre Buffet. The land, however, passed to the state, on condition not only that it be made into a nature reserve and national park, but that the authorities endeavour to restore it to its original ecological state. Consequently there is a small army of marine biologists working on Port-Cros. You may come across them, replanting kelp and other underwater plants. The only access to the beaches is via walkways that are goat tracks at best. There are virtually no cars on the island, and hardly any roads, but it is criss-crossed with a maze of trails and paths, and studded with a handful of massive Napoleonic forts.

As for Le Manoir, this might have been the original inspiration for shabby chic – long before it became a 'look'. It all feels effortless and real. Dinner is served on an outdoor terrace paved in nothing more special than red dirt, but nonetheless set with pink tablecloths, soft green chairs and fine china. The food is fantastic, but served without fuss. A bell announces the early sitting, and you dine with a spectacular view of the sunset over the town's tiny port (seven boats maximum). The venue for breakfast is left to the guests' discretion: choose between the eucalyptus-shaded terrace on the way to the pool, yet another terrace overlooking the island's dense forest, or indeed the same terrace where you had dinner.

The impression created is that you have the island to yourself, and for once that's really not so far from the truth. The daytrippers who come over from the port of Lavandou are obliged by law to leave the island on the last boat. Port staff actually count them in and out, just to make sure. Thus when the last boat has left, the island is completely yours. Should you decide on a late evening stroll to one of the two beaches accessible from the hotel on foot (one a fifteen-minute walk, the other thirty), or a trek through the forest, you will be alone: not an easy status to achieve on the Côte d'Azur. As the proprietor of Le Manoir prefers to say, nature is the attraction here, not people.

---

address Hôtel le Manoir, Ile de Port-Cros 83400, Iles d'Hyères, France

t +33 (0)4 94 05 90 52   **f** +33 (0)4 94 05 90 89

room rates from €160

sofitel palm beach

Alexandre Dumas described the multi-ethnic communities of Marseille in *The Count of Monte Cristo*: 'for three or four centuries they have remained faithful to the little promontory on which they landed, clinging to it like a flock of seagulls, marrying amongst themselves and retaining the habits and dress of their motherland as they have retained its tongue.'

Great literary names and plain old guide books agree: Marseille is a very colourful place. And although it's one of the largest cities in France, it's certainly nowhere near as French as the surrounding environs. Provence is the French countryside with a bit of Italy thrown in, and the Côte d'Azur is France with a Mediterranean flavour, but Marseille is first and foremost Mediterranean. This ancient city, founded by the Greeks 2,600 years ago, bears no resemblance to its neighbours Nice and Cannes. In fact it shares an exotic, African, Arabic ambience with Italian cities like Naples and Palermo that guidebooks, including French ones, tend to pick up on as a vague threat; the place almost invariably gets described as 'risky after dark'. Yet it is exactly this aura that authors and artists have always been attracted to. Dumas chose the city and its smugglers and its rocky *calanques* as the setting for his epic, and even

Asterix and Obelix often visit Marseille as a gateway to their adventures in Sicily, Corsica and North Africa. And whereas other French cities may arrange themselves around a park or a river, Marseille is arranged around a square of salty seawater, the *bassin* of the Vieux Port. Culturally and literally, it faces the Med, with its back turned defiantly to Paris.

Thus nothing could be more characteristic of Marseille than a hotel facing – and preferably on – the water. Situated on the idyllic Kennedy Corniche, with views over the Bay of Marseille, the Isles du Frioul and the legendary Château d'If, it's not surprising that the Accor group invested two years and a substantial amount of money to renovate the hotel now known as the Sofitel Palm Beach. Originally built in the 1970s, it suffered from all the problems that are usually cited by people who bad-mouth Marseille: it was ugly, poorly managed, and its entrance was a regular cause of traffic jams. In fact location was about all it had going for it. But Europe's largest hotel group were not blind to its potential, and they decided to make this one of their showpieces.

The result? An unexpectedly modern hotel that encapsulates all that is good about Marseille. Even locals love it. The restaurant

is a hit, and a popular destination for a weekend lunch. With the advent of affordable regional air travel and a Paris–Marseille TGV rail link, the city is in easy reach of a weekend break from London, Paris, Brussels, Hamburg or Barcelona, to name a few. You can mix lying in the sun and swimming in the Med with venturing into one of the most fascinating urban destinations in Europe, one that's being touted as the next Barcelona.

In architecture and design, the keyword of Sofitel Palm Beach is maritime. When local architects Claire Fatosme and Christian Lefévre took on the task of reinventing the site, they were determined, in their own words, 'to return the hotel to the city' – and by that they also meant to the sea. Everything from the quarried stone floors to the teak planking to the boat-like superstructure of the top floor is expressed in maritime language. Best of all, the interior walls were torn down and repositioned, so that every single guest room now faces the sea. Their decoration continues the theme. Rooms

are fitted in tones of blue, grey and white, with dark wooden joinery in Brazilian ipe, and the restaurant is decorated with massive blow-ups of navigation charts. The most unusual element of the new architecture is that the hotel was turned upside down. The entrance is now on the top floor, level with the high part of the corniche, as is the massive glass and timber lobby. Arriving guests get a fabulous view of the bay, and traffic jams are a thing of the past.

The only thing wrong is the name. This hotel seems too groovy to be a Sofitel. With 160 rooms it obviously does cater to the business traveller, but you wouldn't know it from appearances. Palm Beach invokes the blatant ostentation of America's Palm Beach, which this hotel has nothing in common with at all. The message is confused still further by the fact that there is another Sofitel in Marseille, directly overlooking the Vieux Port. My advice: ignore the name, book a room, and get acquainted with one of Europe's last undiscovered cities.

address   Sofitel Palm Beach Marseille, 200 Corniche JF Kennedy, 13007 Marseille, France

t +33 (0)4 91 16 19 00 **f** +33 (0)4 91 16 19 39 **e** H3485@accor-hotels.com

room rates from €189

villa marie

St Tropez is a circus. With its Russian hookers, Swedish bankers, Italian playboys, American billionaires, Dutch industrialists, Australian sailors, German fleshpots and French celebrities, there is no place in the Mediterranean, French or otherwise, that can match St Tropez for scandal, sex and all-out price-is-no-object exhibitionism. St Tropez, as they, say is *trop*. And that's what has made it a magnet for the summer jetset for over forty years.

Traffic in the high season is almost as bad as London or Paris, prices are even higher, crowds are getting bigger, as are the mega-yachts pretentiously parked along the old fishing port's quay, screaming out 'Look at me, I'm filthy stinking rich'. St Tropez is anything but discreet. Every year the world's travel writers predict that the bubble is about to burst. St Tropez, they say, has finally crossed the line of acceptable gaucheness. Yet every year it becomes more difficult to get a table at Club 55 for lunch and you have to get up earlier and earlier to guarantee a coveted beach parasol. True, the scene is over the top. But that's what makes it so much fun. Shocked, yes, scandalized, perhaps, but you will never, ever be bored here. Besides, what all St Tropez

regulars will tell you is that the scene is there when you want it and when you don't you simply stay poolside at your villa. The problem is of course that not everyone has a villa. Until now, the choice for the St Tropez visitor *sans villa* was some high-profile accommodation in the town itself, such as Byblos or Maison Blanche, or the rustic Moulins on the Route des Plages. For those interested in peace and quiet as well as flash and decadence, the choice was very limited indeed.

There was not just a gap in the market but a huge gaping void, and hoteliers Jean-Louis and Jocelyne Sibuet had been aware of it for quite some time. Having made their name with the now famous Fermes de Marie, Le Lodge Park, Hotel Mont Blanc and Au Coin du Feu in Megève, they knew a thing or two about what the more demanding customers are looking for and what they expect. Thus they were keen to apply their unique formula of quality and character to a summer version of their winter resorts. After many years of looking, they found the ideal property high in the hills, immediately behind St Tropez's famous beaches. By St Tropez standards it was an immense stretch of land: six hectares, blessed with the two most desirable attributes – a view and seclusion.

Jean-Louis knew this was it, and he and his wife did not hesitate to make an offer. The only problem was, the proprietor kept changing his mind. Sometimes it would be for sale, but by the time they got around to negotiating, it was not. For five years the Sibuets played real estate cat and mouse with the owner, who was also the proprietor of all the vineyards as far as the eye could see. But finally the reluctant vendor signed on the dotted line and the Sibuets ended up with not only a prime piece of St Tropez real estate, but more importantly one that already had a hotel on it. Without this, they would have stood little chance of securing the necessary planning permission for their project.

The Sibuets immediately set about putting their signature on the property. To keep the project on track, Jean-Louis and his team of builders and craftsmen moved to St Tropez for two full years. The plan was simple: reorient the rooms to take better advantage of the view, and create interiors evoking the Italian heritage of the area, an aesthetic hybrid of Provençal and Tuscan. The result is a low-key villa – one that creates the impression that it might once have been a more humble farmhouse. It is surrounded by lush gardens that cascade in spectacular fashion down the steep hillside. Fountains, potted fruit trees, imposing wrought-iron gates, cypress pines and olives create a decidedly Mediterranean ambience. Inside the approach continues with plenty of colour – red, orange, green, dark brown – and a particularly eclectic combination of art, objects and furniture that gives the place the feel of an old Italian playboy's villa: drawings by Matisse, Picasso and Cocteau, 1950s patinated garden furniture and the odd gilded Louis XVI piece. The rooms are spacious and unconventional, like mini-Tuscan lofts. Creatively speaking, the hotel is a big success. But perhaps the most telling compliment came from the previous owner who, on a tour of the property just prior to opening, commented rather bitterly: 'If I'd known the rooms had such a view I'd never have sold.'

---

address Villa Marie, Route des Plages, Chemin Val Rian, 83350 Ramatuelle, St Tropez, France

t +33 (0)4 94 97 40 22 **f** +33 (0)4 94 97 37 55 **e** contact@villamarie.fr

room rates from €190

villa mauresque

Dirty Rotten Scoundrels: that's the South of France I had been looking for. If you've seen the film, you will know what I am talking about. Stunning houses, wooden yachts, blue blazers, Hermès scarves and classic English sports cars – bling bling the old-fashioned way. But where is it, I asked myself, as I passed yet another McDonalds, another Carrefour, a Toys'R'Us, a Midas Muffler, a Casino supermarket, and countless service stations. Where are the villas, the immaculate lawns, the glistening swimming pools, the Bulgari-clad socialites, the Benzes and the Bentleys (convertible, of course)?

The answer is that these days it's all hidden behind big gates, guarded by noisy dogs and big, bored security guards. All the interesting stuff on today's Riviera goes on behind closed doors. Wouldn't it be nice, I used to think to myself, if once in a while one of these villas, preferably one with absolute water frontage, could re-emerge as a small, exclusive, exquisite hotel. Then along came the Villa Mauresque. Even from the approach it's promising. The run-of-the-mill security wall has been replaced with a facade straight out of the film *Casablanca*. If the boundary wall looks like this, what must it be like inside?

The answer does not disappoint. Behind the gates, there are two compounds, built in an architectural style best described as 'Moorish oriental folly'. But this is a serious folly, with immaculately sculpted gardens that run right up to the very edge of the Mediterranean. It's the kind of place that leaves most people, particularly Americans, speechless. The rooms are enormous, the view is perfect, and there's a staircase perfectly suited to gliding down in glittering evening dress. There's a swimming pool just outside the dining room, a private dock, a bunch of adult toys (boats, jetskis, kayaks) and another swimming pool (just for a change), all executed in a Moroccan style that is pure Hollywood. Villa Mauresque is a proper Côte d'Azur villa in every respect… except for the fact that it's a hotel.

Not that the proprietors of Villa Mauresque were the first to think of turning an elegant villa in the South of France into a hotel. But most villas that are converted inevitably lose the very quality that was so attractive in the first place. In the quest to expand and invest in additional building, they lose any sense of ever having being a house. That's certainly not the case with this villa. No structural changes were made in order to turn it into a hotel.

Villa Mauresque's suites are all individual; this one is bright, white and distinctly Oriental

Maximum impact, minimum expense – the interiors have been curated with great flair

Right down to the doors, the decorative detailing is completely in step with the villa's Moorish inspiration

Generous windows with panoramic views of the Mediterranean: this is the South of France the way it used to be

Rather than convert all available space into guest rooms, the proprietors preserved the open atmosphere of a villa

Borrow a Bentley and book a few rooms – you and your friends can live your own version of *Dirty Rotten Scoundrels*!

Comprising two splendid houses, one with eight bedrooms, the other five, architecturally this villa is no different today from when it was designed in the 1860s. Neither, it seems, is the lifestyle. Each room is palatial – easily the size of an apartment in London or Milan – with impossibly high ceilings and grand windows straight out of a Fellini film.

My room was a dark green fantasy with an enormous wrought-iron canopy bed. The sun glistening off the calm blue waters of the Med woke me just in time for an early swim before breakfast. I crossed the manicured green lawn and walked to the end of the private jetty via the boat house. There's even a tiny beach (private, of course), but the best swimming is between a cluster of giant rocks just off the property's sea wall. My only regret was that I didn't have my diving goggles. Breakfast that morning was served in the shade, on a deck adjacent to the *belle époque* kitchen and its en suite orangerie, beside swimming pool number one.

It's glamorous, it's beautiful, but in true aristocratic fashion, don't expect everything to be done for you. Like many individual hotels around the world, this is a place that expects you to entertain yourself. Villa Mauresque provides breakfast, but the rest is up to you. You can cook for yourself in the well-equipped kitchen, or go out – maybe take one of the boats and go for a tour of St Raphael, a safe distance from the hoi polloi. Or jump into your Jag and make your way to any number of restaurants (the concierge can help out with an appropriate list). You are close enough to Cannes to park your classic on the Corniche and book for dinner at the Carlton. But the best idea is to leave the grounds as little as possible. Inside the walls of Villa Mauresque you're away from the crowds and the fast food, the shorts and the t-shirts. There's just you, the perfect villa, the immaculate garden and a private slice of the Mediterranean – nothing and no-one to disturb the illusion that the Riviera of film and fantasy does still exist.

---

address La Villa Mauresque, 2 Rue Gustave Eiffel, 33290 Blanquefort, France

t +33 (0)5 56 57 43 94   **f** +33 (0)5 56 57 01 48   **e** contact@villa-mauresque.com

room rates from €131

lugger hotel

The penalty for smuggling in the 1800s was death by hanging. Thus the smugglers who haunted a small inn on the water's edge in tiny Portloe, Cornwall, were taking a not inconsiderable risk in choosing this as their hideaway. In fact, one landlord by the name of Black Dunstan was hanged for smuggling in the 1890s. But Her Majesty's Customs and Excise officers cannot easily have found him. Tucked into a narrow inlet, this waterside hamlet is all but invisible from the water. One has to enter a precariously narrow cove even to catch sight of Portloe, built into a crease between rocky headland and green meadows. Only on the calmest days could one have ventured into such a location with a heavy, clumsy boat powered only by sails.

These days the only real danger in choosing to hide away in this idyllically remote spot on the Cornish coast is sunburn, and maybe melancholy at the thought of having to leave. Tucked away in the very southwestern tip of mother England, Cornwall has managed to maintain its distinct identity by being still so remote (up to five hours by train from London) – that and the fact that until relatively recently there was no real reason to go there. Certainly, by Victorian standards it had little to

recommend it. It was poor, primitive and hotter than the rest of England. Today, of course, the weather, the unspoilt countryside and its remoteness from the capital are precisely why everyone wants to go. Cornwall is hot, and not just with British surfies. The countryside is a vivid expanse of undulating hills and valleys. Then there are the beaches – broad wind-blown sweeps of pale sand framed by mammoth cliffs, the kind that featured in *Chariots of Fire*. And they are pounded by the only decent surf in Great Britain. Some people call it the English Riviera, but the English California might be more accurate.

With so much going for it there is a certain inevitability to the rise of Cornwall as a destination. To a large degree it was Olga Polizzi's Hotel Tresanton in picturesque St Mawes, just along the coast, which pioneered the new chic tourism for Cornwall. The Tresanton is a simple, contemporary place that's abandoned the brass buttons approach to fancy hotels in preference for laid-back lifestyle and a great restaurant. Fittingly, the proprietor of the Lugger was at one time the manager of the Tresanton, and he met his wife when she was staying there as a guest. But whereas St Mawes was already an established vacation town, Portloe is certainly not. The site found by Richard and Sheryl Young (Sheryl is a former London-based banking executive who retired from finance to design the elegantly simple, tastefully contemporary interiors) was not one single building. As well as the inn, it was a collection of tiny stone fishermen's cottages, some dating back to the seventeenth century, arranged higgledy-piggledy around a small stretch of sand that's still used to launch the local fishing fleet. To imagine this as a hideaway for smugglers is one thing, but as a retreat for Mercedes-driving London escapees was another altogether. During the not inconsiderable task of reinventing the property, seemingly mundane questions like 'Where do we put the kitchen?' called for Houdini-like quests of invention, and the hotel's twenty-one guest rooms ended up being divided between no fewer than three different houses. But this inventive, make-do approach only makes the Lugger even more attractive. It's unpredictable and quirky, offering a score of little nooks and crannies and terraces and patios – exactly the kind of spaces people seek on an escape from city life.

If you are staying in England over the summer then Cornwall, most people will agree, is the place to be. And with summer temperatures on the Continent reaching the extremes they have of late, staying in England for the summer is not a bad idea: while the south of France has sweltered and Spain has baked, Cornwall has basked in the balmy but comfortable high-80s. More importantly, Portloe is a place to which you can escape without bringing the crowds with you. While destinations like St Ives and Penzance are quaint, charming and historic, they also tend to fill up in summer with the kind of aimless foot traffic that brings them (like their Continental equivalents such as St Tropez, Capri or Portofino) to an infuriating standstill. Portloe is too small and too unknown to attract crowds. Before the tourists can wreck it, they will have to find it first.

---

address Lugger Hotel, Portloe, Truro, Cornwall TR2 5RD, Great Britain

t +44 (0)1872 501322 **f** +44 (0)1872 501691 **e** office@luggerhotel.com

room rates from £150

katikies

When we think of the Greek islands, we think of blue water, blue sky and simple whitewashed villages twinkling in the sun. The combination of white and azure blue is so Greek that even the nation's flag follows this predominant duotone. But nowhere I have come across takes it to the extreme of Katikies, this cliffside hotel in the picturesque town of Oia (spelled Ía in Greek). The place is literally blindingly white. Without sunglasses, you wouldn't last long here. The steps, the terraces, the roofs, the furniture, the outdoor curtains and cushions, the staff uniforms, the china – everything is white. Contrasted against the deep blue of Santorini's sea and sky, it makes a bold, vivid package.

Katikies is perhaps one of the three most spectacular hotels of the Greek islands. The fact that all three happen to be on the same island does nothing to detract from any of them. But for the sake of clarity, let me differentiate. If complete luxury and complete privacy are your aim, then the Tsitouras Collection is for you. If your taste leans more towards authenticity, beautiful interiors and unpretentious style with an informal attitude, then Perivolas is the place. If, however, you long for a bit of a scene, with a healthy helping of posing and poseurs, then you have to head to Katikies – particularly if you're single. The rooms admittedly don't match the antique-filled eclecticism of Tsitouras, nor do they measure up to the Wilma Flintstone minimalism of Perivolas. But to a degree all that is academic, because Greece is a late-night place. By the time you get to your room the chances are that you will fall asleep face down with your clothes on. It's also true that Katikies is not actually on the beach – though for that matter neither are Tsitouras or Perivolas. But with its low-key minimal dress code, its sunglasses-only brightness, and its colour-scheme typical of a beach house, Katikies is 100% a beach destination even if you never get any sand between your toes.

Still, let's assume you are not the type to hang around the pool, and sand below that bare foot is the aim, after all. Most conveniently located is Baxedes beach, just to the north. It is walking distance and has the added advantage that the 200-odd steps that lead down to it (and back up again) discount any need for further sweating in the gym. The beach also happens to be next door to a small fishing harbour which is home to the Paradhisos Taverna, not a bad place to grab a late lunch.

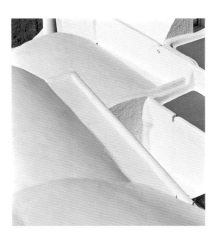

The gleaming whiteness is continually renewed – the surfaces at Katikies are repainted at least once a month

From one of two horizon pools, you can contemplate the possibility that the fabled lost city of Atlantis lies below you

Lunch, and life, are alfresco – with virtually no chance of rain in the summer, every moment is spent outdoors

The hotel's arrangement of space is completely vertical – tiny, winding steps take you up and down the cliff face

The ubiquitous whitewash of Katikies makes it startlingly, blindingly bright – just don't forget your sunglasses

The traditional domed roofs of these cliffside structures have their origins in simple peasant dwellings

Linger over a dish of freshly caught fish or octopus on the terrace overlooking the port and the local fishing fleet. With more adventure in mind, you can rent a boat and head over to the two volcanic islets of Palea Kameni and Nea Kameni, where you can swim in sulphurous mudbaths heated by hot springs.

On Santorini, you can even colour-code your beach itinerary. The island has black beaches, white beaches and even a couple of red beaches. The red is the one that got my attention. Kokkini Ammos (literally red sand) is definitely not walking distance from Katikies, but still certainly worth the effort. Located only a few hundred yards from the ruins of the ancient city of Akrotiri, its red sands framed by red cliffs make a spectacular sight. This southwestern tip of the island offers a more pure, restrained and mythic aspect. The frantic fracas of Fira (Santorini's main town – avoid if you can) is replaced with solitary churches carved into impossibly steep cliff faces. On the way home you can stop at the Glaros Taverna

for lunch and take in the site of Akrotiri before heading back to Oia.

Santorini's legendary beauty is not exactly a best-kept secret, and at the height of the season the cruise ships do tend to hover off its volcanic cliffs. Thankfully, however, the water, right up to the shore, is too deep for them to anchor, so they don't stay long. And even in the busiest months (July and August) it's possible to find complete isolation on nearby Tharissia, whose landscape is untouched by tourism. A short boatride from Katikies, Tharissia has nothing: no shops, no hotels, no bars, no nightclubs, no cruise-ship escapees, just a crystal-blue Aegean, lots of rocks and the odd goat.

Volcanoes, ancient civilizations, age-old trade routes, modern mythology, Santorini has it all – including the fervent belief, which persisted well into the twentieth century, that the island was home to a much feared population of vampires. It's a nice touch. And a perfect excuse never to go to bed.

---

address Katikies, Oia (la) 84702, Santorini (Thíra), Greece

t +30 22860 71401 **f** +30 22860 71129 **e** katikies@otenet.gr

room rates from €260

perivolas

If you long for the simple beauty of the Greek ideal – whitewashed houses, blue doors, the odd red geranium and pathways built for donkeys not cars – then Perivolas is for you. Perched on top of a cliff looking out over Santorini's dark blue water towards the unspoilt island of Thirasia, this is the kind of place you see on the cover of brochures promoting a Greece we all yearn for but which hardly exists in reality. By conventional standards, Perivolas scarcely fits the description of a hotel. It is a collection of individual bungalows (seventeen to be exact) that cascade in a freeform organic fashion down the red and black volcanic cliff faces that distinguish Santorini. Inside and out there's an engaging simplicity to these houses that's completely in sync with the cobalt blue sky and the baking sun.

Not so long ago, Perivolas wasn't a hotel at all. This was a residential area, populated by the poorer citizens of the town of Oia. In the nineteenth century, Oia was a thriving shipping port, home to passing sea captains who plied their trade from Oia to Odessa, Marseille and further afield. Vinsanto, the wine of Santorini, was shipped to Odessa, coal and other goods came from northern Europe. By the time Manos Psychas was born, however, the island's days as

a great seaport were over. But his parentage – Russian mother from Odessa and Greek father from Santorini – remained testament to its one-time cosmopolitan connections. As a child growing up in Odessa, Manos dreamed of travel and the sea, and so it was that he came to command a boat himself. But Captain Psychas also loved the mythical island of Santorini, in particular Oia, perched on its very tip. Over the years, he and his family spent much time there, and thus he decided to buy a series of cave dwellings on the outskirts of town, many of them three centuries old. Local people thought he was crazy. They used these caves, sculpted from the soft volcanic stone, to stable their donkeys. But Captain Psychas was undeterred. He and his wife Nadia adapted these dwellings into houses that are traditionally whitewashed and cubic on the outside, but follow the curved shape of the caves on the inside.

What started as a passion and a hobby turned into a business. By the late 1970s, the Psychas family had more space on their cliff than they needed, and they decided to convert their cottages into a hotel. By the mid-1980s, Santorini was hot. It was being billed as the new Mykonos. Travellers were bewitched by the island's extraordinary topography, just as

Captain Psychas had been back in the 1960s. Perivolas, though small, was the most authentic lodging experience on the island. It still is.

Old Captain Psychas passed away in 1984, but he had a son, Costis, to whom he bequeathed not only his hotel but also his love of the island. Costis Psychas is hardly what you would expect from a Greek hotel owner. Tall, blue-eyed, with a beard and long blond hair, he looks more like a surfer than a hotelier. And as it turns out, he is exactly that – a keen sailor, diver and windsurfer for whom the island is a spiritual home. Costis Psychas has brought to the hotel the street-smart sense of colour and style that is the signature of the surfing world, together with the pared-down approach to accommodation characteristic of the accomplished sailor. Perivolas, as a result, manages to be minimal, cool and colourful, all at the same time. The exteriors are dictated by tradition, but the interiors are a simple, sexy combination of organic shapes, whitewash and fabric in different shades of pink and mauve.

Imagine Wilma Flintstone as a minimalist interior designer, and you get the idea. The cool, cave-like interiors are perfect for the mid-summer heat, but I suspect it's not practicality that pulls the chic French girls in their Chanel bikinis or the Italian men in their boardshorts and boat shoes. It's the look – seamlessly chic and perfectly understated. What's more, the food and service seem as effortless as the design. Simple fare, like the perfect Greek salad or homemade dolmades, is the order of the day. And then there's the not insignificant advantage of a hotel proprietor who is also a man of the sea – here's someone who always knows where to go on the island for a good piece of fish.

But the real draw remains the view. Lots of places on Santorini offer breathtaking vistas, but this one is among the best. Not only is Perivolas very high up, but it also looks directly back over the old town of Oia, down to the deep blue waters of the caldera and across to the virtually uninhabited island of Thirasia. A place to stay? More like a place to dream.

---

address Perivolas, GR 847 02 Oia (Ía), Santorini (Thíra), Greece

t +30 22860 71308 **f** +30 22860 71309 **e** info@perivolas.gr

room rates from €368

the tsitouras collection

Many people believe that the island of Thíra (named after King Thiras of Sparta), or Santorini as it is more often known, is the site of the lost kingdom of Atlantis. In one night 3,500 years ago, this island, a thriving outpost of Minoan civilization, literally sank to the bottom of the ocean. Its volcano erupted with such force that it imploded, tumbling straight down in a pile of dust and rubble, a bit like a skyscraper being demolished, and taking more than half the island with it. The crescent-shaped piece of land that is Santorini today is the volcano's surviving outer rim. The island's steep black and red lava-stone cliffs curve around the caldera, the huge water-filled crater left behind when the volcano's cone collapsed. The explosion would have been heard as far away as Scandinavia. The sheer volume of land displacing sea created a tidal wave many hundreds of feet high that caused devastation as far away as Crete. The ash released into the air would have blacked out a radius of hundreds of miles. Scientists are convinced this was the biggest volcanic eruption in the history of the civilized world.

That a civilization of great sophistication once flourished here is without a doubt. In 1890 German archaeologists discovered beneath the volcanic debris the remains of a city called Akrotiri: streets and streets of buildings (many three or four stories high) with impressive architectural detailing including frescoes and carvings. No bodies or precious items have ever been found here, however, which suggests that the inhabitants had some prior warning and were able to flee before the full catastrophe. Unlike its better known Italian counterparts of Herculaneum and Pompeii, only two per cent of Akrotiri has so far been excavated. But what is uncovered offers plenty of fuel to the Atlantis theory.

This important history may come as a surprise to the average tourist flying in for a bit of scenic sun, ouzo and late-night everything. Santorini visitors do not, by and large, come for the opportunity to visit the ruined city of Akrotiri. And yet it is the island's history that makes the Tsitouras Collection so unique. Dimitris Tsitouras is an Athens-based lawyer as well as an art-lover, historian, author and serious collector, whose hotel celebrates the history and not just the sunshine of Santorini. He fell in love with this island as a teenager, at a time when its volcanic cliffs sported caves, not charming whitewashed houses. He was one of the first from Athens to build a house here,

and in 1985 he was the first to open a hotel of a kind more associated with the south of France than the cliffs of Santorini. Arranged around a generous old villa that has been a post office, a school and a private house since it was built in 1780, and overlooking the caldera, the Tsitouras Collection is aptly named. It is a group of five houses, each designed and decorated with differently themed collections. I stayed in the House of the Winds, a narrow two-storey structure that features a pair of authentic Minoan amphorae rescued from the deep, a bedroom with a blue and gold frescoed ceiling and a bedhead that's a gigantic glass box filled with miniature statues. The property has two marble-clad bathrooms and two vaulted-ceilinged bedrooms, as well as a living room that opens onto a terrace, with superb artworks and artefacts throughout. In short the interiors pay homage to an eclectic and fascinating collection that is, in turn, a testament to the extraordinary history of this island.

Staying at Tsitouras feels just like staying in a house. Not only do you barely notice the staff, but you don't notice the other guests either. The hotel is divided up in such a way that everyone has their own spaces, and unlike a lot of hotels in the Mediterranean, there are thankfully no rules. Breakfast is served where you like, when you like. If you wish to arrange a private dinner on the Maria Callas terrace – no problem. There are no formalities; everything is customized to the individual guest.

So what about the beaches? Sure, Santorini has beaches. You can choose between black-, red- and white-sand beaches, all easily visited in a day. But the greatest thing about Santorini is the view, and for that you need only stay in your hotel. Perched on a cliff face of black volcanic stone, a thousand feet above the deep blue of the Mediterranean, there's nowhere on the planet like it. If you suffer from vertigo, this might not be the place for you. But for most people it's as close as they'll ever get to Mount Olympus, home of the gods.

address The Tsitouras Collection, Firostefani, 84700 Santorini (Thíra), Greece

t +30 22860 23747 **f** +30 22860 23918 **e** reservations@tsitouras.gr

room rates from €620

bommeljé

Windmills, wooden shoes and…windsurfing? Holland is not a place that springs to mind when you think of sun, swimming and sand. Amsterdam for partying, shopping and hanging out – sure. But beach life in the Netherlands? A century ago, however, Holland was an exotic summer destination. British aristocrats on their slim, sexy, wooden yachts certainly thought so. Early yachting journals dedicated entire chapters to the joys of cruising in Holland, with first-hand accounts of flat-bottomed boats, canals, gingerbread houses, black and white Friesian cows, those windmills, and wild and beautiful dunes and beaches.

As travel further afield grows ever easier, particularly within greater Europe, Holland has become distinctly less popular as a summer destination. Yet all the things that used to make the place so culturally distinct are still there. And that includes some very splendid beaches. Holland is on the leeward side of the North Sea, on the receiving end of the prevailing wind. Thus while England's southeastern beaches are flat and muddy, Holland's shoreline is one continuous strip of broad sandy beaches backed by magnificent dunes. In one of the flattest places in the world, these are actually among the country's highest points.

With the exception of Brightonesque resort towns such as Scheveningen, Zandvoort and Noordwijk, the beaches are largely empty and unspoilt. This being Holland, even the most remote sections are easy to access because of a splendid network of immaculately maintained bicycle paths. Most of the dunes are wildlife sanctuaries, so there are no cars, trucks or buses, just bicycles (and mopeds). Few outsiders would know it, but the beach is an established pastime for the Dutch. The Scandinavians have their lakes and their forests and their rocky Baltic islands, the Dutch have their wild, windy beaches. The same wind that has created the sand dunes produces some pretty decent surf, and Holland's North Sea beaches have long been a fixture on the international pro-windsurfing circuit.

Of all the beach destinations in Holland, the most picturesque and unspoilt are those of Zeeland. If it sounds familiar, that's because it was the name given to the antipodean island nation of New Zealand, whose beaches and waterways so reminded Dutch explorers of Zeeland that they called it *Nieuw Zeeland*. Onshore in Zeeland you still find cobblestone streets and gabled houses in small villages with tiny squares and the odd baroque clock in a

church tower. Houses still sport their black and white painted shutters, and bicycles are the preferred way to get around. It's a safe bet that the per capita ownership of small sailboats is close to that of cars, and yes, there are lots of windmills. Some elderly folk still dress in the traditional starched black and white that bears an eerie similarity to the folk dress of Brittany.

Zeeland was and is a popular holiday spot for the Dutch. My Dutch grandparents were regulars to Domburg, which these days is a popular weekend getaway for the chic urban set from Rotterdam, Delft and Amsterdam. Peter Bommeljé was raised in Domburg and his family have long owned a collection of rental apartments there. But despite his small-town background, he is very much part of the new, well-travelled and convincingly urban culture that is the signature of the modern Dutchman. (After all, Domburg is only an hour or so by local train from Brussels.) In order to cater to these new tastes and priorities, he and his wife Marjon decided to turn their apartments into a contemporary hotel. The result, according to Bommeljé's Rotterdam-based designer Agnes Evers, could have pushed the design envelope more. But the restraint was deliberate. The Bommeljés' vision was of a stylish modern interior that would prove a pleasant surprise (not a shock) to guests. This understatement sums up the hotel, the style, the ambience, the location, even the Bommeljés themselves. In Domburg, you won't find DJs in sponsored tents on the beach. In this hotel the most noise comes from the clang of cutlery and the buzz of conversation in the restaurant. The look and feel, despite their modernity, are very Dutch. You will recognize the palette of deep red and sober black and white in just about any painting from Holland's Golden Age. Bommeljé is a contemporary hotel with cultural resonance. And that's the whole point. Cycle through the dunes, sail on old-fashioned flat-bottomed boats, go for *koffie* and *flensjes* on one of the cobbled streets in the town centre. This is a chance to experience beach life the old Dutch way.

address Bommeljé, Herenstraat 24, 4357 AL Domburg, Netherlands
t +31 (0)118 581684 **f** +31 (0)118 582218 **e** bommelje@zeelandnet.nl
room rates from €100

fort tiracol

Goa is India's Florida, the most popular state in the republic for beach getaways. When residents of Delhi, Bangalore, Mumbai and Chennai – the working cities – want to spend some time on a beach, chances are they'll head for Goa. Other states also have beaches – Maharashtra, Tamil Nadu or Kerala – but Goa is famous for them. From the plane, it's easy to see why. The coast is one unending, undulating stretch of sand, hundreds of miles of it, interrupted only by the odd river or rocky headland. Unlike Florida, Goa's beaches are largely empty. Some parts have crowds, it's true, but even then only sporadically. In many places, the only footprints will be your own.

That is certainly the case at Fort Tiracol. Beneath the fort's imposing presence lies a long ribbon of golden sand that ends in a sand bank blessed with a very surfable swell. It is picture postcard material. In a country with a population of a billion plus, it's truly remarkable that something so untouched and undeveloped is possible. Tiracol is the kind of setting that would only be spoilt by a hotel. The thought of any building along this beach is too sad to contemplate. But Fort Tiracol only adds to the perfection. This handsome old Portuguese stone fort could be straight out of

Othello. With a commanding position perfect to capture prevailing winds, it's a one-of-a-kind fantasy, the sort of place you dream of finding and then swear you'll never tell your friends about.

The location is priceless, the setting breathtaking, yet most surprising of all are its interiors: breezily modern in a Terence Conran-goes-to-Brazil kind of way, with a dramatic yellow, black and white colour scheme that reinforces both the building's Portuguese heritage and its Indian location at the very northern tip of Goa, just a stone's throw from the state of Maharashtra. According to the staff, it wasn't always like this. When Claudia and Hari Ajwani found it, the fort was in a shocking condition. The state had spent no money on it, despite its heritage listing, and though it had previously operated as a hotel, it was by all accounts not a particularly salubrious one. My butler Gregory (you get a butler, of course) explained to me that it used to be really quite grubby. 'And,' he said with tremendous pride (and understatement), 'now it's nice and clean. Europeans like it clean.' It's true. Europeans (and Americans) do like it clean. In fact, the staff are so obsessed with keeping it that way that they keep tidying away all the outdoor

furniture the minute a guest has finished sitting on it, much to Hari and Claudia's consternation. It is a bit disconcerting if you only got up to go to the loo.

You don't need to see the 'before' photos to know that the renovation of Fort Tiracol was a giant challenge. But Claudia and Hari are used to this sort of thing. In Goa they are something of a legend, not just because of their other hotel, Nilaya Hermitage, a multi-ethnic organically shaped fantasy in the jungle, but because of the high-calibre clientele they effortlessly seem to attract. Famous film-makers, photographers, actors, writers, fashion people, media and advertising moguls are all regulars. The stars are drawn to Goa's famous beaches and its laid-back lifestyle, and to Claudia's eclectic design skills, but above all what brings people here is that, like André Balazs or Ian Schrager, Claudia and Hari are able to put together a scene. You can arrive alone, but it's highly unlikely that you'll ever eat by yourself. The Claudia and Hari lifestyle

is a sort of salon in the sun, a breezy non-stop round of dinner and drinks set in casual but beautifully detailed surroundings. The secret of their formula is that they make their guests feel good, both physically and (perhaps more importantly) intellectually.

Like many proprietors of interesting and unusual lodgings, they are almost primal in their urge to create. Tiracol was a challenge they couldn't resist, and in the process of fixing it up, they probably set a record for what is possible in India (four months from start to finish). Right now this historic fort is a bit of a best-kept secret. But I predict it won't be long before the crowd that has made Nilaya a regular fixture starts to incorporate Tiracol into their Goa itinerary. And that can only make the place even better. By nature of its very position, this is one destination that cannot be spoilt by mass tourism. Why? Because it's separated from the rest of Goa by a wide, fast-flowing river. The only way across is by a ferry that can take a maximum of three cars...when it's running.

---

address Fort Tiracol, Tiracol, Pernem, Goa

t +91 236 622 7631   **f** +91 832 227 6792   **e** nilaya@sancharnet.in

room rates from US$91

lagoona davina

Imagine this. You arrive at the international airport of Trivandrum (or Thiruvananthapuram to give it its full Malayalam name). You make your way past the throngs who swarm the airport and emerge into the humid heat of Kerala, the southernmost state of India. You are picked up by an Ambassador, the quirkily Indian Karma Cab, and whisked off to the beaches and backwaters that have made this part of India famous since well before Vasco da Gama landed here in 1498. The further you get from the airport, the greener the landscape. Soon the car stops, the bags stay in the trunk, and you are guided down to the water, where a wooden dugout canoe awaits – a canoe shaded by an ornate silver and gold umbrella. The car disappears down the road, and you slide away down a broad river flanked on either side by row upon row of swaying palms, punctuated by the occasional picturesque village. After half an hour or so of seemingly effortless gliding, you hear the sound of the sea. And then the waterway opens into a broad lagoon. On one side is the ocean, on the other is a beach facing the lagoon. You have arrived at Lagoona Davina.

This experience is not so different from that of the Roman, Arab, Chinese and Phoenician traders who came to Kerala in search of ivory and spices as many as three thousand years ago. In later times the Dutch and Portuguese used Kerala as a base for ships carrying spices from Malacca and products from China, en route back to Europe. The locals did not live on the coast (where they risked being washed away by the monsoon floods) so the foreign traders had to venture inland in order to barter for coir, copra, cashew nuts, etc. Winding its way like an intricate web of blood vessels into the interior, Kerala's watery network of lagoons, lakes, canals and rivers was perfectly suited to trade. Centuries of contact exported the culture of southern India to places as far-flung as Indonesia, which is why in Bali, even today, both the architecture (gabled houses built in teak) and the Hindu spirituality are not too dissimilar from Kerala.

Sheltered and protected by mountains and dense forests, this part of India has managed to preserve many of its age-old institutions and customs. Surprisingly, for instance, a visitor from northern India has as much (or little) chance of being understood as a foreigner. Malayalam, the language of Kerala, bears little relation to the national languages of Hindi or Urdu. To communicate, a visiting Rajasthani

must resort to English, the only common tongue. Fishing is still practised from the beach by great teams of men with huge nets. A boat drags the nets beyond the breakwater, and then, in a backbreakingly laborious process, the nets are pulled in by twenty or more men hauling ropes on the beach. It's inefficient, and not always very successful, but it's an ancient ritual complete with chanting such as you are unlikely to witness in many other corners of the globe these days. One of the best places to observe it is the beach adjacent to the lagoon: borrow a dugout and paddle across, or simply swim over. Or you could just sit back under the big shady palms at Lagoona Davina and watch the comings and goings of life on the water as the locals ferry fish, fruit and other produce in precariously laden canoes.

Already when the first Portuguese and Dutch brought back accounts of this pristine coast, virtually every spit and speck of sand along its muddy waterways was inhabited by locals living even then in unimaginable densities. Today Kerala's population is a fat 32 million, so it's hard to believe there's much property left uninhabited. Davina Taylor, the proprietor of this idyllically situated retreat, is quite candid about her extraordinary find. Having travelled through many of India's classic tourist destinations to get here, she knew immediately just how amazing it was. But how did she get here in the first place? What possessed a Londoner to move to India and open a hotel that specializes in healing mind and body through meditation, yoga, reiki and ayurvedic massage? The catalyst came from events in her own life: first divorce and then fifteen years later the collapse of her real estate business. She was drawn to India because it is a very spiritual place. Her children were all grown up, and there was nothing to stop her from staying. And so she did.

That was more than eight years ago. These days the style with which she runs her tiny fiefdom makes it hard to believe it was ever anything but Davina's lagoon.

address Lagoona Davina, TC68/2054 Pachalloor Village, Trivandrum 695 027, Kerala, South India

t +91 471 2380049 **f** +91 471 2382651 **e** lagoonadavina@hotmail.com

room rates from US$58

surya samudra
beach garden

This Kerala beach retreat was the unlikely brainchild of two German adventurers. One, Karl Damschen, is an architect who originally drove all the way to India from Switzerland in the last days that this was safely possible. The other is Klaus Schleusener, a German professor who used to teach at the famous Indian Institute of Technology in Madras, now source of one-third of the brain bank of Silicon Valley, California. In those days, the government of India had closer ties with the USSR than with the USA, and by law foreigners were forbidden from owning real estate. But there were ways around this, and both Karl and Klaus (unbeknown to each other) were looking for the same thing: a choice piece of land on the then virtually undiscovered Kerala coast.

Karl made his way to Kerala from Bombay on a motorbike. Following the coast, he parked his bike not far from where the hotel entrance is today, and proceeded on foot. He had barely stepped onto the secluded beach, empty save for a Christian convent in the adjacent forest of palm trees, when he was informed by locals that a German had just bought the rocky promontory he had been admiring. 'Well, he's a brave man,' was Karl's response. 'It will be very difficult to grow anything on this pile of rocks.'

But fate was cast that day. The two expats met and got along well enough for the professor Klaus to commission a house from architect Karl. And no ordinary house. 'He absolutely wanted an octagon,' says Karl. 'I don't know why, but he was obsessed.' In those days Karl divided his time each year between Bern in Switzerland and Cochin in Kerala. So he produced detailed plans and drawings, with instructions as to materials and methods, and departed for Europe. When he returned to India six months later he was delighted to find the octagon built just as he had envisaged it. The adjacent bathroom, however, was another story. It was huge, almost three times as big as it was supposed to be. Damschen was baffled. How could the same builders get the octagon almost exactly right and yet be so far out on the bathroom? Only when he happened to pick up the tape measure did it finally click. On one side were centimetres (the side used for the octagon), on the other were inches (the side used for the bathroom). The bathroom part was knocked down and done again, and both client and architect learned a lesson in working and building in India's deep south.

The house proved a big hit, as did the idyllic location, and within a short period of

time, Klaus went back to Karl to ask for another house, a place to deposit his many guests. It was an opportunity both of them had been waiting for. Karl Damschen in particular was a great enthusiast for the traditional Kerala teak house, the *tharawad*. It was killing him that these exquisite constructions were being dismantled and sold off as a source of furniture timber. Karl's advice to Klaus was, 'See if you can buy a traditional Kerala home, and we will work out a way to re-erect it on the property.'

The next time he visited, he was met by Klaus bearing a large grin. 'Look at that pile of timbers,' said Klaus. Neatly numbered and sequentially packaged, there were not just one but several teak houses awaiting resurrection. And that was not the end of it. More houses followed, accompanied by more landscaping, until the decision to turn the private compound into a small exclusive hotel became a natural next step. Facilities were basic compared to what they are today. There was no pool, no phones in the rooms, no water filtration system

and no real restaurant. But none of it mattered. It was (and still is) a place of tremendous charm – a magnificently secluded hideaway.

Surya Samudra has changed a lot since then. There's a beautiful new pool carved into the rocks, a comprehensive ayurvedic spa, and the garden has matured almost beyond recognition. Klaus has moved on, replaced by an Indian company, though Karl remains involved as an architectural adviser. But the most dramatic change has neither to do with progress nor new management. Thirteen years ago, Surya Samudra had one big sandy beach to the left, facing out to the Arabian Sea, and a tiny one to the right. Today the tiny beach is no longer. It's been replaced by a beach far bigger even than the one next door. Locals see it as a divine omen: the gods are happy. But for me it's a wonderful example of the fleeting nature of beauty. Two years ago, the beach didn't exist, until a particularly persistent monsoon brought it here – but another monsoon could just as easily take it away again.

address Surya Samudra Beach Garden, Pulinkudi, Mullur P.O., Trivandrum 695 521, Kerala, India
t +91 471 2267333 **f** +91 471 2267124 **e** info@suryasamudra.com
room rates from €120

hotel le dune

Blame Ryanair, Go and EasyJet. Until recently, many corners of Europe remained surprisingly remote and unexplored. Northern Germany, southern Sweden, eastern Italy, western France, Carcassonne, Toulouse, Lisbon, Stockholm, Palermo – these places were not high on anyone's list of must-sees because, frankly, the option of flying there wasn't an option. Then discount airlines hit on the idea of using regional airports. And hey presto, Europe opened up like a multi-layered jewelry box.

But is this bad? Has it spoilt things for the handful of more adventurous travellers who perhaps might have considered places like Italy's Puglia their own special secret? Maybe. But in most ways it's the opposite of bad. Limited tourism can ensure that places like Corsica or Campania don't die out, economically speaking. Because with no other option, the people of such remote areas inevitably move to the city. More to the point, the expansion of exploration within Europe actually brings with it its own brake on tourist development. With so many options, and more emerging almost daily, it becomes ever less likely that any of these new destinations will suffer the fate of the Costa Brava. By spreading the tourist load, airlines such as Go, EasyJet and Ryanair are stimulating sustainable tourism.

One of the beneficiaries of this new pan-European democratization of travel has been Sardinia. The thing about Sardinia is that with the exception of the Costa Smeralda in the north, and the odd Forte development in the south, most of the island has remained untouched by travel and tourism. In particular, its wild west coast, with magnificent sand dunes and all but deserted shores, is largely unknown. If you are flying into Olbia to spend a week or so at the exquisite Hotel Cala di Volpe, why would you leave to make an excursion to an area you know practically nothing about? You just wouldn't, which is why Sardinia's west coast has remained an extraordinarily well-kept secret. Those Milanese and Romans who are in on the secret fly to Cagliari, rent a car and drive northwest for a couple of hours, but until recently the rest of Europe and the world was effectively shut out. Now that Ryanair flies to Alghero, however, the dunes of Sardinia's west coast are a potential escape destination for anyone living within range of London's airports.

In rather Machiavellian style, the greatest strength of this awe-inspiring coast is also its greatest weakness. It's a stretch of beach of the kind we all dream of, wild, untouched, *sauvage*.

Nothing but dunes, sands and water. And that's the point. There's nothing here: no villages, no towns, no shopping, no cafés, no restaurants, not even any roads…with one exception. Follow an old unpaved mining road for long enough and you will eventually spy the dramatic dunes of Piscinas that lay claim to being the largest expanse of desert in Europe. The same road winds its way down to the sea past many abandoned buildings that testify to this area's past as a centre for mining galena and sphalerite. When you reach the water the scenery changes from a rugged but slightly sad and industrially tainted landscape to a vista of sand dunes that stretch as far as the eye can see, framed by the crashing foam of an endless beach. There are no harbours or ports or tiny towns to interrupt the seemingly infinite view of sand, sand and more sand.

There's only one building on the beach, and it is virtually unavoidable because the road stops here. When the mine was active, this was the loading shed for the ore that would arrive in wagons pulled by ponies. Today it's Hotel le Dune. When its owners took on the property, the mine was long closed, and the land in most people's estimation was next to worthless. Yet despite its atmosphere of abandonment, they understood its potential as an escape destination. As a hotel, Le Dune is nothing glamorous. The rooms are spacious, clean and modern, but they will never win prizes for decorative sophistication. The lobby living area is cosy, with a big open fire in the winter – but it's cosy in a rugged, worker's pub kind of way. The restaurant is not impressive furniture-wise, but that's more than made up for by the fact that it's directly on the beach. Indeed, the overwhelming attraction of Le Dune is its location. Stranded like a piece of driftwood on a seemingly endless beach that fades into an undulating series of substantial dunes, this is a place where you can easily forget crowded, civilized, cultured Europe. Here you can experience a coastal wilderness without having to travel halfway round the world to find it.

address Hotel le Dune, Via Bau 1, Fraz. Piscinas di Ingurtosu, 09030 Arbus, Cagliari, Sardinia

t +39 070 977 130   **f** +39 070 977 230   **e** info@leduneingurtosu.com

room rates from €45

hotel raya

It's almost impossible to come across an article about Italian fashion duo Dolce and Gabbana without some shots of their holiday home on the volcanic island of Stromboli. They talk about it in glowing terms; they use it for fashion shoots and to entertain superstar friends. In a word, they have done what fashion people do – they have made the Aeolian islands fashionable.

Salina, Lipari, Vulcano, Stromboli, Panarea: not so long ago this handful of remote islands was among the poorest parts of Italy. The inhabitants were either farmers or fishermen and the struggle to make a living was such that a significant percentage of Aeolians migrated to Australia and the United States. But it was inevitable that the post-war search for sea, sun and sand would eventually lead to these idyllic little isles located a day's boat ride north of Sicily and a day's boat ride south of Naples. The first to kickstart a wider awareness was Roberto Rossellini, who made the film *Stromboli* starring Ingrid Bergman in the late 1950s. Three decades later, another classically romantic Italian film had even more people asking: 'Where is that place? I want to go'.

That place was Salina and the film was *Il Postino*. By that time, people in the know – or at least Italians in the know – had already discovered the Aeolian islands. Architects, film makers, actors and industrialists had built houses there and worked hard at keeping their retreat as unfêted as possible. The Costa Smeralda and Portofino had the 'scene'; the Aeolian islands had the opposite – no scene, no crowds, no tourism. With the arrival of the likes of Dolce and Gabbana, however, it is unlikely that these islands will ever now return to their humble roots. Perverse though it may sound, your best bet these days is a smaller and less attractive island. Panarea does not have the verdant mountains of Salina, nor Stromboli's dramatic volcano and black sand beaches. It is small, slightly hilly, and sparsely developed. There is no building over two stories high, and the consistent architecture and colour scheme of its small cubic houses suggest that it is a place that tourism has passed by.

In truth, Panarea's aesthetic is entirely a recent invention. When Paolo Tilche and Miriam Beltrami first disembarked in the 1960s, Panarea was virtually abandoned. But Tilche and Beltrami saw only potential in an island with bay after pretty bay and beach after unspoilt beach. Plus, the island has a perfect view of Stromboli's active volcano. Paolo Tilche had spent time on the Greek island of Hydra,

one of the first Mediterranean islands to adopt a strict code in building styles and colours, as well as in traffic management. So it is thanks to him that today Panarea has no cars, no trucks, no buses, no motorcycles and – thank God – no mopeds. Bicycles and feet are the order of the day, and as if to emphasize the permanence of the code, most of the island's roads are no wider than the girth of two donkeys.

This is a destination perfectly art-directed for the pursuit of simple pleasures. You wake, wander down to the small harbour town, have a coffee, and when you are ready take a mid-morning stroll to a small secluded beach of your choice, past gleaming white houses with their Mediterranean blue doors and burnt orange detail (the only two colours allowed). By contemporary standards, Panarea really does check all the boxes for the perfect escape. It is a tiny hedonist's paradise.

A lucky few, mainly from Milan, have houses here. And then there's the itinerant summer crowd who arrive on yachts fully equipped to cruise the abundance of small bays and beaches. The good news for visitors *sans* house or yacht is that the entrepreneur behind the island's aesthetic reinvention presciently reserved the premier slice of real estate for his hotel. Impeccably whitewashed, immaculately minimal, with flashes of exotic Balinese colour, Hotel Raya is completely in step with the island's unaffected lifestyle. Architecturally, the conception of Raya was a masterstroke. The pavilion that houses the bar and restaurant is on a natural plateau just above the village and harbour, looking straight at Stromboli. The guest rooms, by contrast, are on the other side of town, tucked into the island's rocky foothills away from all the activity, yet still only a five-minute walk from the restaurant and bar. This clean break between privacy and participation is one of Raya's unique luxuries. The other is Panarea itself. Dolce and Gabbana may be directly under Stromboli's spectacular volcano, but those are the cheap seats. The royal box is a table at Hotel Raya.

---

address Hotel Raya, Via San Pietro, 98050 Panarea, Italy

t +39 090 983013 **f** +39 090 983103 **e** info@hotelraya.it

room rates from €186

round hill

A former sugar plantation on the outskirts of Montego Bay, Round Hill is where Jacqueline and J.F.K. spent their honeymoon; where Oscar Hammerstein and Richard Rodgers played chess; where Hitchcock got sunburned; where Noel Coward, if egged on enough, would sing for the guests. Bing Crosby, Bob Hope, Errol Flynn, Paul Newman, the Aga Khan, Charlie Chaplin…the list goes on and on and on. In a competition for name-dropping, there are few hotels in the world that could take on Round Hill. Even today the celebrity stakes are high. Stella McCartney, according to staff, practically grew up here, while Beatle dad Paul would play dominoes with the locals, who didn't give a damn if he was a Beatle as long as he could play (dominoes, that is). And whereas Noel Coward was the celebrity most identified with Round Hill in the past, now it's Ralph Lauren and family who have become the new glamour fixture. From November on Lauren is here almost every weekend. With only three hours' flight time, it's quicker to fly from Manhattan to Montego Bay than to drive to the Hamptons. (Though it does help to have your own jet.)

Just what is it about Round Hill that makes it such a magnet, particularly for people utterly spoilt for choice? A significant part of the equation is Jamaica itself. Jamaicans will remind you that they are a nation, not just an island; a nation of three million, with cities and highways and crime and shopping centres and its own very particular culture. Jamaicans are open, friendly, very laid-back, and have a wicked sense of humour. One thing they are not is remotely impressed by fame and celebrity.

But the warmth of the people aside, the success of Round Hill goes back to fifty years ago, when a young Jamaican laid down the blueprint for his development. John Pringle was from one of the island's oldest and most privileged colonial families. He'd been living and working in New York, but for some inexplicable reason he was obsessed with returning to Jamaica to open a hotel. The fact that he had no hotel experience, nor any money to speak of, did not deter him. Through family connections he was made aware of a piece of land about half an hour's drive from the centre of Montego Bay. It was part of a large cattle and farming estate, but this gently sloping rounded plot (hence Round Hill) wasn't exactly stellar in agricultural terms. That of course suited Pringle perfectly because he was mainly interested in the little beach at the end of the site.

His mother paid the deposit, but otherwise Pringle had to resort to imagination to finance his dream. A plan was hatched with his lawyer: he would parcel off a twenty-five-acre tract to house the hotel and twenty-nine cottages that he could sell off-plan. The revenue generated by the sale of the cottages would pay for the hotel. It was devilishly daring, and it worked – beyond any of Pringle's expectations. His success was boosted immeasurably by the fact that the first sale was to none other than Noel Coward. Although Coward was a friend of his mother, Pringle had never himself met him. But by chance he found himself sitting next to Coward on a flight to New York. Seizing his opportunity, he pulled out drawings and photos of the Round Hill site and spent the flight pitching the scheme. Eventually Coward put his hand on Pringle's knee and said, 'My dear boy, if you will only stop boring me I'll buy one of your blasted cottages.' True to his word, he did.

Having the illustrious Mr Coward as his first client was a huge coup, and it opened the floodgates. So much so that one American magnate agreed to buy a plot on the basis of a photo for a price of £25,000, enough to finance all the real estate in one hit. In fact, by the time the Paleys heard about it, there were really no cottages left. But nobody said no to Bill Paley, the Murdoch of his day, so Pringle blasted a site from an adjacent cliff and built the fantasy of a house that is today owned by Ralph Lauren.

After fifty years Round Hill has a million stories to tell. But the most impressive is how little it has changed. In a world obsessed with technology and driven by built-in obsolescence, it's exciting to come across a place that savours its uncomplicated authenticity. There's nothing flash about Round Hill, and there never has been. The place today offers the same blend of qualities that has always pulled the famous names and faces, namely a well-preserved slice of old Jamaica, with sympathetic architecture and a predictably colonial pace of life: lunch at one, tea at four, dinner at eight and lots of swimming, snorkelling and sailing in between.

address Round Hill, P.O. Box 64, Montego Bay, Jamaica, West Indies

t +1 876 956 7050 **f** +1 876 956 7505 **e** info@roundhilljamaica.com

room rates from US$260

soneva gili

One thousand, one hundred and ninety green, blue and white, amoeba-shaped islands floating in a crystal-clear sea just north of the equator – the Maldives are like nowhere else on the planet. From a plane it seems impossible that these exquisite sprinkles of palm trees, coral and sand could be inhabited. They seem so fragile. And in fact they are. As the sea is rising, the Maldives are sinking. With a maximum height above sea level of seven feet, climate change was already such a concern that the government of the Maldives struck a deal with Australia several decades ago. Should the 250,000-odd Maldivians be in imminent danger of losing their homeland to the sea, the Australian government committed to allow them to resettle in Oz. Biblical but true.

Aside from being a few inches lower in the water, this gentle but strict Islamic republic has changed little since H.C.P. Bell, the British Ceylon commissioner, travelled to the Maldives in 1879 to detail the contents of a shipwreck. He ended up staying and was eventually to become *the* expert on the Maldives, author of a definitive monograph on the history, archaeology and epigraphy of the islands. 'See a Maldive atoll and die – 'tis beauty truly bent,' he wrote. It's true most islanders no longer fish or trade coconuts for a living, but the islands' beauty remains undimmed. It may even be enhanced: Lord Bell never had the opportunity to see them from the air.

Enchanting as these islands are, it is their underwater beauty that attracts many of today's visitors. The diving and snorkelling in the Maldives are among the best in the world. Even though a greater portion of the reef is being bleached by global warming, there is still plenty of colour and spectacle left. Wildly striped and polka-dotted tropical fish, gropers, schools of baby sharks – these translucent waters are like the world's biggest aquarium. Being a hair's breadth from the equator doesn't hurt either. The weather is always warm, and so is the water, but ocean breezes ensure that temperatures are hardly ever extreme.

The Maldives are most people's idea of paradise. Except that until recently, paradise was a pain in the neck to get to. It inevitably involved a flight to the Middle East, followed by a long wait in the airport, followed by a further five-hour flight to Malé, capital of the Maldives. And even then you still had to make your way to your respective island. New airlines and new direct flights have changed all that. So the only decision left is which of 1,190 islands to go to.

The government has helped your choice. To contain the impact of tourism, only ninety-odd islands are allowed to host holiday-makers. The rest are strictly off-limits. Island-hopping is also discouraged, though with the atoll being so stretched out, the chances are that the island you stay on will be the only one you'll visit. This puts a lot of pressure on each resort. It must sustain visitors' interest without compromising the qualities they came for in the first place.

What's required is an approach that Sonu Shivdasani and his wife Eva (hence Soneva) describe as 'intelligent luxury'. What they mean by this, in a nutshell, is the art of being spoilt without spoiling anything else, whether environment, culture or people. At Soneva Gili, pampering is done with such devotion that it's almost like religion. But it's not what you think. It's not about supplying endless stacks of fluffy towels or extending happy hour at the bar. It's about using creativity, imagination and design to create a new experience. To start with, there are no rooms at Soneva Gili. Guests each get

their own villa extending over three levels, with an open-plan living area, a small kitchen, a bedroom, a huge bathroom with private water garden and a roof terrace. Best of all, each villa has its own swimming platform, which is possible because all of them are built on stilts directly in the lagoon. Some stand right out in the water and can only be reached by canoe. Even the spa complex and the hotel bar are on the water. Only the restaurant, the dive school, the boutiques and reception area are on land.

Cynics might point out that cottages on stilts are nothing new, but there is an intelligent and innovative approach to the architecture at Soneva Gili that is. Even taking a shower is an experience when your shower is a glass block cylinder suspended ten feet above the lagoon, and the only way to reach it is via a small bridge. The island has plenty of white powdery beaches, but Soneva Gili's accommodation solution goes one better. To sample some of the world's best snorkelling all you need do is slip off your own swimming platform.

---

address Soneva Gili Resort & Spa, Lankanfushi Island, North Malé Atoll, Republic of Maldives

t +960 440 304 **f** +960 440 305 **e** sonresa@sonevagili.com.mv

room rates from US$675

deseo

They call it the Riviera Maya, a 230-mile-long ribbon of perfect white sand that stretches from Cancun on the easternmost point of the Yucatan peninsula to the border with Belize. About a third of the way down lie the ruins of Tulum, once a major base of Mayan civilization. Unlike other Mayan cities such as Chichen Itza or Tikal, Tulum (or Zama as it was known until a few hundred years ago) is not set deep into the jungle. Its collection of temples, meeting halls and palaces stand on the highest point along the entire coast, surrounded by palm trees and beaches of super-fine coral sand, like talcum powder. Dating from 1200 AD, these structures in the famously distinct pyramid form, with a square top and reverse sheer walls, were exclusively for the ruling Mayan elite. The remainder of the population lived in simple wooden dwellings with thatched roofs not unlike the structures used for the beach clubs of nearby Playa del Carmen.

By building this city right on the beach, the Mayans who dominated the Yucatan peninsula set a precedent that's now being taken up with gusto by millions of snowbirds – northern Europeans and Americans desperate to escape the winter snow, sleet and slush of their own countries. Cancun is the most famous

destination in this part of Mexico, but despite beautiful beaches, it's not to everyone's taste. From the air it looks like Miami, Acapulco or Australia's Gold Coast – rows and rows of gargantuan hotels built right on the beach. Add to this a population that's now approaching a million and it is understandable why real travellers have started venturing further down the coast.

Less than twenty years ago, Playa del Carmen was a small fishing town thirty minutes from Tulum. It had a beautiful broad stretch of perfect white sand and no tourists, yet was under an hour from Cancun's airport. It was discovered by Italians and accordingly came to be developed more in the mould of Positano than Cancun. Playa today is not exactly a small fishing village, but neither is it the Las Vegas-style high-rise strip that Cancun has become. In short, it's a happening little town with lots of energy. The beach is never more than a block away, and the streets (pedestrian traffic only) are chock-a-block with cafés, restaurants, bars and shops. During the day, everyone is on the beach, at beach clubs that have a lot in common with those of St Tropez. You rent a bed under a small thatched palapa, you have lunch at your club, and then when the sun

goes down everyone heads back to town to participate in the evening *passeggiata*, or *paseo* as it's known in Spanish.

Playa del Carmen is fun and sexy, and it's easy to understand why it's still so popular with Italians. But what it didn't have until the arrival of Deseo was an architectural equivalent of its exuberant energy. Most of the buildings in town are funny hybrids – a bit of concrete, the odd colourfully painted wall, and the occasional roof of thatch. I like palapas – they are original to the region, and they look good on the beach. But placing a thatched roof on a concrete building in town is like wearing a baseball cap to Royal Ascot. Deseo is the way it should all be: modern, fresh, but still unmistakably Mexican. Above all, it's completely in sync with the laid-back lifestyle of the Riviera Maya. Situated in the centre of town, yet only one block from the beach, Deseo is a smaller, gentler and more private version of the hotel-as-nightclub phenomenon kickstarted by Ian Schrager in places like LA

and Miami. Arranged around a courtyard that is raised one storey above street level (a bit like being on top of a small pyramid) the rooms are open-plan lofts painted ice blue, equipped with big frosted glass doors that can slide open to expose you to the bar, the pool and the outside beds that account for the 'lounge' part of the full name, Deseo [Hotel + Lounge]. Guests can linger around the pool, order snacks from the small breakfast bar, and meet for drinks in the evening to listen to the DJ's selection.

It's the art of lounging as perfected by the proprietors Carlos Couturier and Moises, Rafael and Jaime Micha. After making quite a splash with their Mexico City hotel Habita, the team have brought their heady mix of cutting-edge modernity and laid-back lounging to the Yucatan Peninsula. Relaxed and low-key, Deseo is the perfect place to hang out. But don't be fooled by the casual atmosphere. This is a hotel of rigorous and refined detailing, a showcase for stylishly and successfully cutting with convention…without charging a fortune.

---

address Deseo [Hotel +Lounge], 5a Avenue y Calle 12, Playa del Carmen, Quintana Roo 77710, Mexico

t +52 984 879 3620 **f** +52 984 879 3621 **e** info@hoteldeseo.com

room rates from US$138

hotelito desconocido

Only an Italian could create a place like this. Hotelito Desconocido – literally 'Undiscovered Little Hotel' – is surely the most romantic place in Mexico, if not all of the Americas. The setting couldn't be more seductive. Hotelito's thatched *palafitos* are arranged along a broad lagoon flanked by mountains and palm forests on one side and by a massive virgin beach and the booming surf of the Pacific on the other. The lagoon is home to an extraordinary variety of wildlife, including herons, vultures and pelicans, and each year hundreds of newly hatched *tortugas* (turtles) start their voyage to maturity by making their way across this beach and into the wild surf.

As you pass through the nearby *pueblo* – a place straight out of *El Mariachi* – and descend towards the distant palm trees that tell you the Pacific is not far away, nothing can compete with your first glimpse of this palm-fringed lagoon and its long strip of unending beach. It was this view that prompted Marcello Murzilli to put his life on hold and embark on one of the most ambitious escape destinations I have come across. He first saw the lagoon from the air. He was flying from Careyes just to the south, itself the pioneer of a whole new approach to Pacific development, reintroducing

indigenous sensitivity in palm-thatched palapas built without steel, concrete or glass. As he swooped across the 8-mile long lagoon, the only one along a 49-mile stretch of unbroken sand, Murzilli knew he just had to have a closer look. There were no roads to where he wanted to go, so he hired some *charros* on horseback with machetes, and off they went. When they finally reached the lagoon, like a modern version of Cortes' little band of conquerors, he knew then and there that this was the place where he could realize a dream.

The locals were bemused by this unshaven man with holes in his shirt and a knotted handkerchief on his head, especially when he started making enquiries about buying the land. To people who lived from farming, fishing and ranching, he must have seemed a complete madman. And maybe he was. But he was also creative, persistent, entrepreneurial and, despite appearances, rich. Marcello Murzilli had a jeans company called (ironically enough) Charro, which he sold up after twenty years of hard work, leaving behind a life of helicopters, big business and Formula One sponsorship (yes, really) to restore a wooden yacht and sail around the world for two years. It was during this time that he rethought his life philosophy.

Authentic, colourful and captivating –
Desconocido's architecture makes a
beautiful place even more beautiful

Powerful Pacific waves crash on the
hotel's perfect beach, an unspoilt stretch
of sand only accessible by boat

Each individual palafito has a theme
inspired by Mexican village bingo –
this one, in green, is *El Pino*

The endless deserted beach and the palm-fringed lagoon are Hotelito Desconocido's star attractions

Built from mud and dried palm fronds, and painted in traditional colours, the palafitos are authentic inside and out

Bright red, candy pink, canary yellow, jungle green and Frida Kahlo blue make up the decorative palette of Desconocido

'Once you have every toy and thing you could imagine,' he will tell you, 'the ultimate is to have nothing. To enjoy nature in her pure unspoilt state – to go to bed when it's dark and to wake up when it's light. To enjoy the simple pleasure of candlelight every day, and to do without computers, cars, newspapers, telephones or television.'

While the village was still scratching its collective head, the Italian with the holes in his shirt had already bought the land and rapidly become the area's biggest employer. Up to two hundred workers toiled for four years. Roads were laid, jungle was cleared, palm trees were planted and lots of buildings went up – none of them like anything else along this coast. Murzilli insisted on building the accommodation in the style and manner of original Mexican dwellings. These palafitos are shacks on stilts made of palm fronds and mud, with roofs of trimmed branches and palm-leaf thatch. Painted bright yellow, they may be authentic but they are anything but plain or

basic. They are all different, all wonderfully eccentric, vividly colourful and hopelessly romantic. The interiors ingeniously follow the colours and themes of Mexican bingo. Some are pink, others blue or green or yellow, with impressive four-poster beds swathed in mosquito netting, doors and windows made of woven palm, outdoor showers, bathrooms with colourful tiles, oiled wooden floors, and a riot of naive oil paintings on the walls. And of course, because there is no electricity (just solar power by day), there are lots and lots of candles in all sorts of containers, pots and lamps.

While the palafitos were being built, along with two bars and two restaurants, reception, spa and stables, Marcello Murzilli lived on the beach in a tent. As he talks of those years, you can see from the twinkle in his eye just how special they were. There was much hardship, much expense and many setbacks, but the result speaks for itself. Only an Italian could take a place this beautiful and make it even more so.

address Hotelito Desconocido, Playon de Mismaloya, Jalisco, Mexico
t +52 322 281 4010   **f** +52 322 281 4130   **e** hotelito@hotelito.com
room rates from US$260

the chedi

Be honest. What do you know about the Sultanate of Oman? Chances are, your answer will be 'very little'. But that's OK, because until relatively recently Oman was the hermit of the Middle East. Once the region's most powerful empire, with colonies as far-flung as Zanzibar, and lucrative trading connections with India, China and Europe, Oman by the beginning of the twentieth century had lost its independence to Britain and its wealth and influence were greatly diminished. Economic downturn went hand in hand with political change. No sooner had Sultan Said bin Taimur come to power in 1932 than he began to impose a reactionary programme of isolation. A once expansive empire regressed into a medieval torpor. Travel was forbidden, even within the country. Education was suppressed, and the few exit visas allowed were issued by the Sultan himself. Anything vaguely representative of the West was summarily banned. Imports of radios, books, even eyeglasses were illegal. For forty-odd years, Oman was effectively shut out.

Said bin Taimur was overthrown by his son Qaboos in 1970. Thirty years old when he came to power, the Sandhurst-educated Sultan Qaboos bin Said surrounded himself with British advisers and set about lifting his father's dire restrictions and modernizing the country's economy. But the apple, as they say, never falls far from the tree. In developing his country, he too has demonstrated a passion for preserving Oman's traditional character. For example government employees are required by law to wear traditional dress at work: for men, a *dishdasha* (floor-length shirt dress, almost always a pale purple) with a *wizar* (a type of sarong worn underneath) and the optional *khanjar* (curved dagger); and for women, a more colourful *dishdasha*, *lihaff* (veil) and *sirwal* (baggy trousers gathered at the ankles). Construction of modern office blocks in the capital Muscat has been confined to certain areas. The city's old port, site of the Sultan's palace, has few shops, no hotels, and retains its age-old Arabian aesthetic. Outside Muscat, life goes on virtually unchanged (albeit with better health care and education). The family remains the cultural core, with anything up to fifteen children not uncommon; water is still fetched from a well in rural villages; and marriage outside one's village is almost unheard of. People have televisions and cars, but modern conveniences do not seem to have affected their way of life. Even the nomadic tribes who have long since settled elsewhere in the Middle East still roam parts of the interior.

For the traveller, this is all good news. Here you can experience the traditions, the customs and the atmosphere of the Middle East as they were before the spending power of oil money changed everything. Oman too has some income from oil, but nothing like as much as its neighbours. Most surprisingly, the country is not the barren sandy place with the odd date palm that we imagine of the Arabian peninsula. Oman has mountains – real mountains, with 9774-foot Jebal Akhdar as its highest peak. In the south, where the plains and mountains of Dhofar catch the monsoon, the landscape is surprisingly lush and green, particularly in August and September. If you insist on romping in sand dunes, however, Oman can more than accommodate. Wahiba Sands in the north boasts some of the most spectacular dunes in the Middle East, and camel or four-wheel drive expeditions are regularly organized. And when it comes to beaches, Oman has more to offer than any other nation on the Arabian Peninsula. Most of the country's thousand-mile coastline faces the Arabian Sea not the Gulf, meaning its endless white sand beaches have a tropical feel.

Given all this, it's little wonder that the Singapore-based GHM Group chose Oman for their latest instalment of evocative, design-led hotel architecture. Borrowing from a tradition of famed Bedouin hospitality, the Chedi offers a more personal alternative to the cluster of large five-star international hotels in Muscat. Its architectural profile is like that of a handful of traditional Arabic villas. Its style is a streamlined and modernized version of Omani vernacular. With the added benefit of distinctly affordable prices for such unashamed luxury, you can while away the day at two different pools or on the immaculate private beach, or head into town to shop at one of the finest souks in the Middle East. While neighbouring Dubai offers a flashy gold-chain-and-Gucci version of the Middle East, the Chedi Muscat gives you Lawrence of Arabia…without the tent.

---

address   The Chedi, North Ghubra 232, Way No. 3215, Street No. 46, Muscat, Sultanate of Oman

t +968 52 44 00   **f** +968 50 44 85   **e** chedimuscat@ghmhotels.com

room rates from RO63

beachcomber resort

The thatched hut on stilts in a blue lagoon has become as much a part of any South Pacific paradise as coconut oil and grass skirts. In any case you don't have much choice: Japanese honeymoon couples insist on it. That's why the lagoon of Bora Bora now counts more than eight hundred huts on stilts, belonging to half a dozen or more luxury hotels. The appeal is easy to understand. You have the luxury of your own private house, and to snorkel in one of the world's most perfect lagoons all you need to do is slip off a platform. So ubiquitous are these huts on stilts that you could easily imagine that they have always been part of the scene. In fact, they are entirely the result of some creative and relatively recent real estate development.

The story starts in the early 1960s with a trio of young Californians, known in these parts as the Bali Hai Boys, who virtually invented Polynesian tourism. Long before it became fashionable to drop out, this group of American businessmen – lawyer Hugh Kelly, stockbroker Jay Carlisle and salesman Muk McCallum – opted for a more laid-back life in paradise. But grown-up beach bums need to make money, and so they turned to tourism. Saddled with property on the island of Moorea that was not

remarkable for its beaches (as in, it had none) they conceived a series of individual bungalows built over the lagoon. This way they could offer swimming without actually needing a beach. The only snag was getting it past the French authorities, who are not exactly known for their flexibility or imagination. To do this they pitched their scheme as a heritage project, arguing that the natives of French Polynesia once would have fished from exactly such a platform. Natives, of course, didn't have bathrooms, electricity or hot and cold running water, but the argument was sufficiently plausible to win them the official go-ahead. Thus in 1966, way ahead of anyone else, six bungalows were built. The concept was quick to take hold. A couple of decades later it was refined by the invention of the aquarium coffee table, a glass table on top of a glass plate inserted into the floor which gives honeymooners a fish's-eye view of the natural aquarium beneath them, without getting wet. This lagoon-viewing development was followed by another innovation: the canoe breakfast, delivered by a Polynesian outrigger powered by paddling natives festooned with flowers.

Not everyone, it should be said, is entirely happy about some of the world's most beautiful

waters being turned into a Robinson Crusoe version of an offshore oil field. But Tahiti has always inspired both awe and disillusionment. Even Paul Gauguin, 150 years ago, found its capital, Papeete, too busy and commercial, with the harbour overcrowded, the town too bustling, and precious little to offer in terms of pure Polynesia. Today it's much the same story, only more so: big airport, big harbour, lots of touristy shops. But you have to fly into somewhere, and that's the role the main island of Tahiti plays. Most flights land at two or three in the morning, so an immediate connecting flight is not really on the cards. After a few days' recovery, a local flight of forty-five minutes will get you to Bora Bora. Small airport, mesmerizingly blue lagoon, dark green volcanic mountain and a few private yachts: Bora Bora is a totally different story. All its resorts can only be reached by boat, like Venice. And in truth, the island is easily big enough to absorb the several hundred huts on stilts that dot its shores. Your speedboat

is hardly weaving in and out of them as you make your way along the bay. For once, the water, the sky and the overall scenery are exactly like the brochure – except better, because the scale here is so unexpectedly large. The lagoon is immense, and the mountainous mainland dwarfs its little huts.

Which brings us to the question, once in paradise, which one do you choose? The Sofitel Bora Bora, the Hotel Bora Bora, etc. – to be perfectly truthful, they are *all* beautiful. But Intercontinental's Beachcomber Resort has the edge thanks to its location on Matira Point. Not only does it have a splendid beach, sheltered from the prevailing winds and so perfect for swimming, but it is also the last hotel on the lagoon, giving it an added seclusion. The huts are in a vast area, all of which is both deep enough to swim and shallow enough to stand up. Snorkelling and swimming are what the Bora Bora experience is all about, and for that the Beachcomber Resort has the best position.

---

address Beachcomber Resort Bora Bora, BP 156 Vaitape, Bora Bora, 98730, French Polynesia

t +689 604 900 **f** +689 604 999 **e** borabora@interconti.com

room rates from €609

quinta do caracol

Not too long ago this was João Marcelo Viegas's grandfather's farm. Tourism had not come to Tavira, and this part of the Portuguese coast, much closer to the blossoming Andalucian city of Seville than to Lisbon, was home to farmers and fishermen.

Tavira today has some tourism, but thankfully the region has managed to hang on to its historic livelihood, and visitors are an additional form of income rather than an alternative. Tavira's charm is that it falls into a kind of geographical gap: too far for convenient access from the Costa del Sol and the Costa de la Luz, especially if you are flying in on EasyJet, and also too far from mainstream Algarve destinations for most Portugal-bound sunseekers to find their way here. The lack of crowds and the absence of mass tourism suit people who frequent Tavira very well, particularly those lucky enough to end up at Quinta do Caracol.

It may have been Viegas's grandfather's farm, but today Quinta do Caracol is more like a luxurious ranch than a farm. Painted in the traditional colours of Portuguese peasant houses – blue, yellow, white and a dash of pink – it's the kind of place you see in magazines but never seem to find in real life. With a

handsome driveway lined by sizeable date palms, and organically curved whitewashed architecture, Quinta's appearance is both startling and seductive. But the aesthetic is only the starting point of its appeal. If maintenance were an Olympic sport, Viegas would win a gold medal. The plants are immaculate, the whitewash is pristine, the paving stones are dust- and blemish-free, and the interiors are spotless and generous in terms of both space and facilities. In fact, the guest accommodation has little more in common with a standard hotel than a nightly room rate. Each guest apartment is more like a mini-farmhouse, with small kitchen, large bathroom and the odd corridor connecting separate dining, living and sleeping areas – a comfortable largesse not at all reflected in the price, which is surprisingly affordable. Wherever possible, Viegas has preserved the interior features that clearly tell you this was once an old farmhouse: for example the floor-to-ceiling fireplace that provides an extra place to sleep in one apartment, or the private roof terrace that was once a lookout. History and tradition are employed as design ingredients throughout the interior. Furniture is plain and simple, as you would expect in a farmhouse, with the odd

antique or family heirloom, whether it be a nineteenth-century English polished mahogany chest of drawers or pieces of the old family porcelain hanging on the walls.

But enough about the colour and the plants and the plates and the Portuguese grandpa. This is a book about beaches, so what's the beach like? Given that this was once a farm, it's clear (or should be) that Quinta do Caracol is not right on the beach. But then neither is any of Tavira. Because this is a fishing town, the fleet is sheltered in a canal hidden behind the coast's wild sand dunes. All the beaches are thus outside of town, and the best ones are on the outskirts of the neighbouring town of Santa Luzia. Going to the beach in Tavira is a decidedly odd experience. Not more than a five-minute drive from Quinta do Caracol, the road takes you past the palm-lined fishing boat canal and stops a bit further along by a small pedestrian bridge. At which point, I might add, the beach is nowhere to be seen. I followed the hotel's instructions to the letter, and yet I ended up at a dead end, stranded in a wetland with some sand dunes in the far distance.

None of it made any sense until the train turned up – a small turn-of-the-century number that would be equally at home on a pre-World War II Swiss skiing slope. You jump on with your boogie board and your towel, and it zips you across the marsh straight to a perfectly unspoilt beach. Of course it's unspoilt, because apart from taking this tiny choochoo there is no other way to get there.

Not that making your way to the coast on a Willy Wonka train is mandatory to enjoy Quinta do Caracol. Back at the farm, there's a clay tennis court (immaculately maintained, of course), stables with horses and a perfect circular swimming pool. Design-wise there is nothing cutting edge about Quinta do Caracol's seven spacious suites, but then there doesn't need to be. They are cosy, handsome and authentic. Perhaps most importantly, the place looks and feels like Portugal – which in a world of EasyJet tourism is increasingly hard to find.

address Quinta do Caracol, 8800-405 Tavira, Algarve, Portugal

t +351 281 322 475 **f** +351 281 323 175 **e** quintadocaracol@mail.telepac.pt

room rates from €50

hix island house

It all started with Hurricane Hugo. After years of vacationing on the quiet Puerto Rican island of Vieques, Toronto-based architect John Hix had finally purchased his dream piece of land – thirteen hilltop acres of Vieques's tropical jungle with panoramic views of the Caribbean. As Hugo hit the headlines, the builders were ready, but Hix had not submitted working plans. According to meteorologists, the hurricane would miss Vieques…but it didn't. Hix stayed up all night glued to the TV following its progress. It was a wake-up call. He literally went back to the drawing board to design a house that could withstand a hurricane.

The triangle, as Hix will tell you, is the strongest shape in nature, and so a triangular house it was – in reinforced concrete with enormous cutouts to maximize the view, and strategically placed metal roll-down shutters in case another tropical tempest should come along. Hix also decided to leave the outside raw and unpainted. What he created was both practically and aesthetically a tropical bunker – a poignant design direction in light of the island's recent history. Vieques, a twenty-minute flight from Puerto Rico's capital San Juan, didn't used to be much of a tourist destination. That's because most of the island

served as a base for the United States navy, who used it for combat exercise and shooting practice. Even the beaches of Vieques were codenamed for wargames, hence Red Beach, Blue Beach, Purple Beach, Green Beach, etc. It was paradise wasted. The locals certainly thought so: the navy's presence was highly unpopular, and whenever they could, the citizens of Vieques would venture out in little boats and enter restricted zones just to make their message felt. Even the island's mayor did a stretch in the brig. In the end it was a tragic accident that triggered the US forces to pull up stakes. A navy employee was killed when he left his bunker for a smoke during bombing exercises. When the navy departed, it handed over to the American forest and wildlife authority, who turned the entire area of the base into the largest wildlife reserve in the Caribbean. Which is great news for travellers, because it means none of the island's unspoilt beaches are available for development – not a house, not a hotel, not even a snack shack. The beaches are as they should be: totally empty.

As so often with highly individual places, Hix Island House was never planned as a hotel. It evolved into one because John Hix figured it was high time some of his friends started to pay.

Owner-architect John Hix has designed sophisticated spaces perfectly suited to a tropical environment

Towering blade-like walls that alternately hide and reveal tropical vistas are one of many modernist tricks used at the house

Design details at Hix Island House are pervasively linear, like this floating day bed suspended by stainless-steel cables

Intersecting planes highlighted by dramatic shadow – the visual intricacy is a treat for photographers

The massive concrete walls and panoramic cutouts of the loft-like spaces combine enclosure and exposure

DIY Rietveldt. A design classic made from marine ply – simple and affordable, just as modern design was meant to be

The luxury of the interior is in the space, the location and the view rather than the raw materials

All of the loft-like studios are in raw concrete, except for this single room rendered in adobe-coloured wash

Bathrooms are stylishly composed of thick slabs of polished concrete – powerful geometry in the tropics

Without the surrounding dense greenery, the expanses of bare concrete could have been depressing

There's nothing conventionally Caribbean about these Philippe Starck armchairs and angle-poise tripod lamps

The monochromatic calm of concrete floors, walls and ceilings is interrupted only by vivid Marimekko bedspreads

The first of John Hix's hurricane-proof buildings was based on the triangle, the strongest geometrical shape

The cleverly conceived studios feel as if they are open to the elements, yet during a storm the bed will remain dry

A studio entrance ascends through a two-storey void. This is an architecture of ritual and drama

Like a true bunker, Hix Island House is almost entirely hidden by the surrounding jungle

Massive architectural cutouts bring tropical breezes and views of the jungle into the pared-down interiors

Formerly the site of a huge US naval base, Vieques is home to the biggest wildlife reserve in the Caribbean

So he built more villas, each in his signature bunker style. At first glance, the suites of Hix Island House have more in common with a big city loft than a Caribbean island hideaway. Yet these open-plan shapes, with polished concrete floors and huge unglazed cutouts framing postcard views, are perfect for the tropics. The building's design allows the reliable trade winds to circulate, eliminating the need for air-conditioning. Which is typical of the ecologically sensitive spirit of Hix Island House. Electricity is generated by solar panels, the water from the showers irrigates the lush tropical fruit garden, and the handsomely designed swimming pool uses a low-chemical cleaning system.

The impression created by these Caribbean lofts is that of being on a boat, and at night it's like sleeping on deck. The architecture blurs the distinction between outside and inside. One end of your loft is exposed to the elements, yet your bed is far enough inside never to get wet. You can experience a tropical downpour without closing a single window – there are none. Hix Island House is the tropics amplified by modern architecture and design. It's not just that each loft is around four times the size of a typical hotel room, but the sense of space is boosted by the openness to the elements. It's all about visual sensation – a far more sophisticated tool than merely fluffy towels or Frette linens (though you do get these too).

A certain sort of rugged simplicity asserts itself with the fact that the hotel has no room service, no restaurant, no café and no bar. The message is clear. We give you a great space to stay, you entertain and feed yourself. Each suite has a fully equipped kitchen and a well-stocked fridge, and the bread delivered to your room each morning is baked fresh on the premises. The hotel is run by a couple who have both done their fair share of globetrotting. They will give you directions to the island's most remote beaches at the drop of a hat, but they are not likely to send into town for your favourite painkiller or designer vodka. This, after all, is no place for princesses.

address Hix Island House, HC-02 Box 14902, Vieques, Puerto Rico 00765

t +1 787 741 2302 **f** +1 787 741 2797 **e** info@hixislandhouse.com

room rates from US$190

north island

Normally when designers take on the task of creating paradise, the first thing they add is palm trees. The more palm trees the better. North Island must be the first resort in the world where the plan is the reverse: to uproot as many palm trees as possible.

They call it the 'Noah's Ark' concept. The intention is to restore this island in the Seychelles to its pristine state, turning back the environmental clock two hundred years. But how, you might ask, can it not be pristine? These are the Seychelles, tiny tropical packages of green water, blue sky, white sand, verdant jungle – what's not pristine about that? Well, despite the unrivalled beauty, these islands have plenty of interlopers: rats, wildcats, cows and pigs, as well as palm and casuarina trees. None of these are indigenous to the island. They might look like part of the natural order, but in fact they are all imports, and as such they endanger native species and threaten the islands' delicate ecosystem. So although it may seem excessive to plan to uproot almost half the vegetation and replace it with more than 100,000 indigenous plants, keep in mind that the developers and architects of North Island are on a mission. They intend to make North Island authentic with a capital A.

The visionary team behind this project includes Wilderness Safaris, who also manage a collection of award-winning private bush camps in Africa. Together with architects Silvio Rech and Lesley Carstens, they were determined to create somewhere that would be more than just a scenic setting for baking in the sun. Their approach is founded on two key convictions: one, that tourism can be fostered without wrecking a place, and two, that it can be used to repair or even restore the damage. Imagine such a thing! Appropriate development might one day restore the beauty and charm of the Costa Brava, Rhodes, Acapulco, Mazatlan, Queensland's Gold Coast and all the other places that tourism has defaced beyond recognition.

Once a coconut plantation, North Island had been uninhabited for some thirty years before the new owners came on the scene. After such a long period of abandonment, they jumped right in and did…nothing. For years, they simply took turns to visit the island, camping out for a couple of weeks and getting acquainted with the lie of the land, the prevailing winds, the best beaches, etc. This was a process continued by the architects when they joined the project in 1998.

Husband and wife team Rech and Carstens call it an 'architecture of experiences'. It's true, theirs is a highly individual approach. Part of their design philosophy includes living on site. They moved onto North Island in 2001 accompanied by their son Gio, who had spent some of the earliest months of his life at the Ngoro Ngoro Crater Lodge (the so-called 'Masai Versailles', one of the couple's previous design successes), and their daughter Luna, born just three months before. To set up a tent and take note of weather and wind is one thing, but to move to an abandoned island with a child and a tiny baby…Rech and Carstens also describe their work as 'adventure architecture', and with good reason.

North Island wasn't so much created as nurtured − gently coaxed to maturity with an inordinate amount of attention. The eleven guest villas, each with a roof of traditional *alang alang* thatch, were built by a team of craftsmen from Africa, Zanzibar, Bali and the Seychelles. More thought went into the door handles here than most hotel projects get in total. But this is not the result of runaway enthusiasm or manic egocentricity. The overwhelming attention to detail is part of a planned process which the architects are convinced enhances the feeling of escape. 'When you travel halfway round the world from an urban environment such as New York or London,' they argue, 'you don't want the taps or the sinks or the furniture or the lamps to be anything you recognize. You want them to be "island-like", whatever that may be.' Rech feels deeply that it's their responsibility as architects never to allow the lack of detail to spoil the dream.

The whole North Island experience was designed to be exactly that − an experience. Its purpose is to reconnect us with the tides, the elements, the sun, the moon, the joy of eating on a beach under the stars or swimming by moonlight as white-tipped sharks circle about. It's an experience designed to strike a primal chord.

---

address North Island, Seychelles

t +248 293 100 **f** +248 293 150 **e** info@north-island.com

room rates from €2190

birkenhead house

The Cape, most South Africans will tell you, bears little relation to the reality of Africa. The political struggles, the medical crises and the financial challenges of the continent don't seem to have travelled this far south. People here go to the beach, drink wine, dine out and generally enjoy the Cape of Good Hope equivalent of a Mediterranean lifestyle. So what's wrong with that? Well it's fiddling on the roof as Rome burns as far as much of Africa is concerned.

It's true, the southernmost tip of South Africa lives in isolation – splendid isolation. Few places on earth can boast the many graces of Cape Town and environs: theatrical mountainscapes, fertile green valleys and of course countless sandy white beaches. South Africa's Cape is like the rich kid at school who has it all and yet is also infuriatingly charming and unspoilt. Capetonians are dismissed by Jo'burg urbanites as fools in paradise, but this is no different from the attitude of São Paulo residents to the beach bums of Rio, or New Yorkers' disdain for California's unending sunshine. Here's a city with a 3,520-foot mountain in the middle (Table Mountain), Dutch and British colonial architecture, an engagingly restored waterfront and a café, bar, bookshop or brasserie on every other corner.

What outsiders don't realize is that Cape Town's personality as a modern hedonistic society of clubbers and beach-goers is not the result of the city ignoring recent changes, but of embracing them. Freed not just from the racism of the country's white rulers, but from their antiquated, church-going, God-fearing lifestyles, the city is finally starting to make the best of what it had in its backyard all along. No wonder the number of international flights landing at Cape Town airport has more than doubled in the past ten years. As one journalist wrote, 'the sheer weight of things going for it crushes resistance.' Swimming, surfing, kloofing (a South African version of canyoning), gliding, skydiving, sandboarding, sea kayaking, wine tasting, bird watching, whale watching…the Cape is like a Chinese menu of travel hedonism.

But if you are really searching for the Cape of Africa, the place that's truly like nowhere else on earth, then you need to head on out of Cape Town. You might venture towards the Breede River Valley and the Overberg, in the same direction that the Trek Boers (migrating farmers) took to escape the urbanization of Kaapstadt and the unpalatable prospect of British rule. It's here, in the homesteads of the winelands, that Cape Dutch architecture came into its own. These gabled, whitewashed structures are a three-dimensional expression of their builders' transplanted culture, a northern European aesthetic expressed in a more relaxed and temperate manner.

The coastline south of Cape Town is a wild combination of big empty beaches and rust-coloured rocky mountains, and it offers a safari-like array of marine wildlife, including African penguins, the Cape fur seal and bottleneck dolphins. If you are game you can cage-dive with sharks; less daring but no less cinematic is the opportunity to watch whales. Hermanus, a former fishing village 75 miles southeast of Cape Town, is one of the best places in the world for whale watching. Every year between June and November the southern right whale (*eubalaena australis*) comes to Hermanus's Walker Bay to calve. The creatures come so close to shore that they can be viewed from the beach, and there can be as many as seventy in the bay at a time. But the best place to watch them is from the stylish platform built into the cliffs above two

of the town's best beaches, location of Birkenhead House. The hotel is named after the infamous HMS Birkenhead, which sank off the coast in 1852 taking 454 souls with her. It's a slightly odd choice of name – unless perhaps you consider that the hotel sits like a shipwreck on the oceanside cliffs. The star quality of this hotel is obviously its spectacular position. The décor, in deference to the setting, is cosily eclectic, an accumulation of bits and pieces from overseas and the odd antique, just as you might expect of a family beach house – which makes sense given that it was originally the holiday home of proprietors Phil and Liz Biden.

Watch whales, dive with sharks, walk along the beach to the old fishing port, visit award-winning wineries built in the Cape Dutch style, or never leave this stunningly situated hideout, savouring the fact that January and February here are the height of summer instead of the deep, dark depths of winter. This is a beach hotel for people who do not have to go on safari to convince themselves they are in Africa.

address Birkenhead House, 7th Avenue, Voelklip, Hermanus 7200, South Africa

t +27 28 314 8000 **f** +27 28 314 1208 **e** info@birkenheadhouse.com

room rates from R3800

100% fun

With a name like this, there's a lot to live up to. At the very least you'd expect Hotel 100% Fun to be…fun. And it is. How could it not be, located bang opposite one of Europe's most spectacular beaches, a vast stretch of sand that ends in huge sweeping dunes. And then there's the wind – plenty of wind. In fact, the wind is so reliable that Tarifa's beaches have become one of the ultimate kiteboarding and windsurfing destinations in the world, on a level with Maui's Hookipa Beach or Oregon's Hood River.

Tarifa's Los Lances Beach is a surfers' paradise. It bears no resemblance to the sad, crowded little strips of sand on the over-developed Costa del Sol. Indeed, it has more in common with Sydney's Northern Beaches than with any other part of Spain's coastline. Which helps to account for the fact that the hotel's proprietor is an Aussie expat. Barry Pussell is a Sydneysider who can only be described as a sports nut – a surfer and a keen sailor who became a ski instructor in Australia and moonlighted as a board-shaper. These days he's put his board-shaping behind him and he concentrates on his golf. Amazingly (or perhaps not) he's good enough to have recently turned pro. Surfing, windsurfing, sailing, skiing and now golf! When, you might ask, does he get

any time for hotelling? But that's not even all he does. Somehow, some way, he finds the time to run a shop, a restaurant and a board-manufacturing business as well.

The hotel was originally not even part of the masterplan. When they first took up residence here, Barry and his wife Ula started a shaping business (his) and a shop (hers). A half-Danish, half-Swiss native of Madrid, Ula met Barry while they were both working as ski instructors in the Austrian Alps. After a short stint in New Zealand and Australia they moved to Madrid – but Barry hated it. Inevitably, perhaps, they ended up on the beach, where they were among the first to recognize the potential of this wild and beautiful piece of Spanish coastline. As a mad keen windsurfer as well as a talented shaper, Barry did what most shapers do: surf when the conditions are ideal, shape when they are not. He made the boards while Ula looked after the shop and the kids. It was only logical that the same people who bought the boards and the gear in the shop might also need a place to stay, and so Barry and Ula decided to add 100% Fun the hotel to 100% Fun the shop. And of course surfers need to eat. So they created a restaurant in a large thatched open

hut in the middle of the compound. The food? TexMex. As every serious surfer knows, in a place created by surfers for surfers, it couldn't possibly be anything else. TexMex is to a surfer what a curry is to a British pub-crawler.

Another consequence of being conceived by people who know the culture is that this is a hotel without corridors. Corridors for windsurfers are death. What do you do with dripping wetsuits, boards, sails, etc? At 100% Fun, every room is a bungalow with its own terrace, perfect for drying all the gear. And they are, almost without exception, on the ground floor – much easier for dragging your equipment back and forth from the beach. To provide a measure of privacy, the bungalows are set in a lush tropical garden complete with fountains, ponds and tribal sculptures. The interiors are relatively simple but attractive nonetheless. Ula Pussell opted for a palette of bright Mexican colours as the main decorative ingredient. All in all, with its Polynesian thatched hut sheltering a TexMex restaurant,

a tropical garden and scattered primitive art, it's a mad mix of ethnic influences – which is perfect, because it's precisely such cultural borrowing that has always defined the aesthetics of the surfing world.

The shop, the restaurant, the kitesurfing school, the custom-made boards: is this the perfect surfers' retreat? Of course it is. But it's still a lot of fun if you don't surf. There used to be a saying among surfers: 'if you surf, never stop – if you don't…never start.' It's a lifestyle that's not looking for new recruits. Quite the opposite. Surfers are loath to share any information about their waves, their beaches, and, in this case, their hotel. They are like the Freemasons of the sporting world. So all the better when you as a non-surfer stumble upon one of their sacrosanct hideouts. It's a chance to savour a colourful and sexy lifestyle without having to commit to eating TexMex for the rest of your life, or having to add numbingly repetitive words like 'awesome' to your vocabulary…dude.

---

address 100% Fun Hotel, Ctra. Cadiz-Malaga Km.76, 11380 Tarifa (CA), Spain

t +34 956 680 330   **f** +34 956 680 013   **e** 100x100@tnet.es

room rates from €75

the beach house

Andalucia, once the heartland of the highly cultivated Moorish empire, is the most Spanish part of Spain. This is the deep south, birthplace of Flamenco, home to whitewashed villages, terracotta pots filled with olive oil, and spectacular remnants of Moorish splendour such as the Alhambra in Granada and the great mosque in Cordoba. It's also blessed with more sun than most other parts of Europe. Which is why the coastline has become famous in its own right as the Costa del Sol. Marbella, Torremolinos, Mijas and the like are collectively one of Europe's biggest magnets for sunseeking northerners.

Magnet it may be, but the airport in Malaga is not a good start. It's shiny, new, modern and a touch tacky (maybe it's the walk through an enormous fake aquarium on the way to claiming your baggage). Architecturally speaking, it has nothing particularly Spanish, let alone Andalucian, about it. And it's an omen for worse to come. As I drive along the Costa del Sol's sweeping eight-lane motorway past a mini-metropolis of high-rise, Hong Kong-like apartment blocks dominating and sometimes entirely blocking the view of the glistening Mediterranean, I can't help but imagine what this stretch of coast looked like before it

became the most popular second-home destination for Brits in Europe. Admittedly, the real estate boom in the south has helped make Spain one of the richest nations in the EU today. And major public works such as Seville's train station and countless bridges, some designed by celebrated sculptor-architect-engineer Santiago Calatrava, have added some poetic modernity to Andalucia. But this cannot be said of Malaga in particular or the Costa del Sol in general. However, most people who jump on an unquestionably convenient and affordable EasyJet flight from the UK are not in search of architectural masterpieces. Sun, sea and sand are sufficient attractions. The sheer number of visitors has created an extraordinary infrastructure. Any kind of cuisine you can think of is available – Chinese, Thai, Lebanese, Moroccan, French, Italian – and the same is true of the shopping. You may not like the look of the place, but you won't get bored.

Among all this towering concrete, something eventually had to emerge of a style and scale that would appeal to a different kind of traveller. The Beach House is an enigma – a villa fronting a private stretch of beach with no surrounding tower blocks, less than twenty minutes out of Malaga. How is this possible, you might ask?

I didn't believe it either. Particularly not after the drive past high-rise after high-rise, concrete town after concrete town. There was not a single break in all this development until I reached the village of La Cala. Here there are no towers, just houses with absolute beach front. The only tricky bit is finding the access road that runs alongside the motorway, but once I did, the Beach House virtually presented itself. From the outside there's not much to see, just a big wooden gate and a discreet sign. The gate slides back to reveal a parking area and an elegant doorway tiled in a Moorish manner, which opens to the villa's interior, its courtyard and the beach beyond. It's a newly built property, but in detail and layout, the entire villa follows Andalucian tradition. Centred around a courtyard with floors tiled in the *zillij* pattern of Moorish mosaic, the architecture retains the inward-looking serenity of a courtyard-based riad, and although it is not grand in scale, the view straight out to sea creates a feeling of immense spaciousness.

With just nine rooms, you never have to share the beach with too many others. The Beach House is small, serene and chic – the opposite of the nearby sprawl.

These immaculate chocolate brown and white interiors are the work of a Scandinavian designer who now lives on the Costa del Sol. Kjell Sporrang owns an interior design business in Sweden, but the opportunity to express his signature style on the southern Spanish coast was a challenge too good to turn down. It was such a success that in the end he decided to stay and help run the place. The proprietors, like Sporrang, are also Swedish, and the Beach House is an expression of what they wanted – but couldn't find – in southern Spain. Their efforts were fuelled by the confidence that it would be a success because it would appeal to people just like them. By word of mouth alone the Beach House has earned a steady, loyal clientele. Why? Because it offers the convenience of Malaga with the ambience of somewhere completely different.

address The Beach House, Urb: El Chaparral, CN. 340 km 203, 29648 Mijas Costa, Spain

t +34 95 249 45 40 **f** +34 95 249 45 40 **e** info@beachhouse.nu

room rates from €140

la sacristía

If you happen to be an architect who surfs, or a kitesurfer who designs, this is the place for you. La Sacristía is exactly how one would imagine a place in the deep south of Andalucia: exotic, mysterious, steeped in history and tinged with a strong Moorish influence. What one perhaps doesn't anticipate is a level of sophistication on a par with the best-designed hotels in world cities like New York, London and Paris. There are no bright surfer colours anywhere in this small, ten-room hotel – unless you count the odd gilded icon on a wall, or a low Japanese-style bed painted a handsome dark red. The interior is also not the whitewashed cliché that is so omnipresent in this neck of the woods. Instead, all the walls are a restrained and quite unexpected shade of fawn grey, the colour of their unpainted render. Rooms, corridors, café, shop and restaurant are unified by this single colour scheme, which imposes a tremendous calm on the historic building, a former inn in the old walled quarter of Tarifa dating back to the seventeenth century.

Colour may be uniform and spare, but the interiors are anything but plain or simple. Their beauty and diversity come mainly from clever use of space. Each room is entirely different, and each room is distinguished by a special antique: a Venetian mirror, an extraordinary bed, a beautiful lantern, a red Chinese lacquered cupboard, an English chair upholstered in a slinky damask, a heavy pair of Castillian wedding beds, etc. These very select pieces make such an impact because the interiors are otherwise so restrained.

The other thing all the rooms share is a tremendous sense of spaciousness, which perhaps reflects the fact that one of the proprietors, architect Miguel Arregui, used to design interiors for Oberoi resorts in India. 'Space to breathe and a place for peace' is how Arregui and fellow designer-proprietor Bosco Herrero sum up their creation. In a hyped-up surf town like Tarifa, they have a point. There are more surf shops here than on Bondi Beach. The prevailing aesthetic is strictly surfer: bright colours and ethnic twists, sandals, cargo pants, screen-printed t-shirts, bleached blond hair, and lots of beads and shark's-tooth pendants. Much as you may love the sport – surfing, kitesurfing, windsurfing – that doesn't necessarily mean you want to spend the night in a surf-themed bedroom. Even golfers don't do that. The arrival of La Sacristía provides a calm, pared-down, architecturally sophisticated accommodation option in Tarifa.

The surfing scene gives Tarifa its energy and vibrancy, and the weather (or rather the wind) gives it its reputation as one of the top destinations for windsurfing, but it is Tarifa's history that makes it unique. Thirty minutes across the water lies Tangier, Morocco's most notorious city, whose lights are visible by night. The strategically situated, massively reinforced city of Tarifa remained a skirmish point between Moors and Christians long after the rest of Spain had capitulated to the Castillians from the north. But the town's rich history goes still further back. The cove of Bolonia, tipped by Tarifa locals as the most stunning beach in the area, was once the backdrop to the thriving Roman town of Baelo Claudia (named for Emperor Claudius, AD 41–54, who granted it the prestigious rank of municipality). Baelo Claudia owed its wealth to the production of garum, the fermented fish sauce that Romans ate with everything. Made from fish intestines mixed with salt, oil and lemon, Baelo Claudia's garum was exported all over the empire, and the success of the town's factory on the beach afforded its 3,000 residents a privileged lifestyle. The thirteen-hectare city, surrounded by a massive protective wall, boasted a forum, four temples, a theatre, baths, gardens, market, pharmacy, tavern and basilica. However, its prosperity was brought to an abrupt end in the second century by an earthquake, whose effects are still visible today in the buckled paving stones that line the streets. Abandoned in the sixth century, it remained untouched (except as a handy source of building materials) until the late 1960s, when work began in earnest to uncover its well-preserved ruins. Being in one of the more remote stretches of Spain was a blessing: before the tourism crush could spread to this unspoilt quarter, the government declared most of the area a national park.

So here's the twist for the style-savvy surfer. Stay in a 300-year-old Moorish villa inside the old town walls at night, and surf during the day just yards from the splendid ruins of an ancient Roman town. Who says surfers are a-cultural?

address La Sacristía, San Donato 8, 11380 Tarifa, Cádiz, Spain

t +34 956 681 759 **f** +34 956 685 182 **e** tarifa@lasacristia.net

room rates from €115

ada

Purely by coincidence, my arrival at Ada coincided with the celebration of Turkish independence. This was the first day of modern Turkey (or Türkiye, as they call it here), the official end of the Ottoman Empire and all its faded imperial pretentions. In its heyday, the Ottoman Empire reached from Morocco to Persia, north to the borders of modern Russia and as far west as Austria. At one point the Ottoman Turks were pounding on the gates of Vienna. These powerful military conquerors were descendants of the fiery Huns of Chinese Mongolia. But they were also culturally articulate. In architecture and handcraft, the Ottoman Empire was prolific, consistent and of lasting impact. Like most great civilizations, it had its proud and its not so proud moments, but it left a substantial and meaningful legacy.

It was precisely this Ottoman legacy that former Turkish industrialist turned tourism entrepreneur Vedat Semiz sought to invoke when building his hotel in the idyllic seaside town of Türkbükü, on the Bodrum peninsula. A chemical engineer by training, Semiz started his working life with ICI and later left to build up his own polymer technologies company. He eventually sold out once his company had become Turkey's market leader. Semiz clearly

has all the energy and zeal of his Ottoman forefathers, and he is passionate about all that he tackles. One of his passions is the rich archaeology of his nation. He is a serious collector of artefacts from all periods of Turkish history – from the ancient Greek and Roman settlements to Christian Byzantine civilization to the unique aesthetic of the Islamic Ottoman Empire. Until quite recently, Turkey's government preferred to turn its back on the past, discouraging any celebration of Ottoman achievements. Yet aesthetically it was a rich period packed with visual detail worth revisiting, and it provided the basic blueprint for Ada.

Semiz's vision was of a luxurious retreat capitalizing on Türkbükü's enchanting location while recalling various aspects of Turkey's cultural–historical legacy. It helped, of course, that he had the financial resources to realize his vision, not to mention a collection from which the project could draw. Like many people whose success is self-made, he knew exactly what he wanted and, just as important, exactly what he didn't want. The brief to the architects was not only to design in the local style, but to use local materials, particularly stone, in such a way that the building would blend in with its surroundings.

Texture, patina, the appeal of the handmade – Ada's interiors have a timeless quality, despite being brand new

Bold, heroic and authentic, Ada was never meant to be just a hotel; it is a celebration of Turkey's cultural heritage

Ada is a stunning stylistic hybrid mixing local materials, historic pieces and a casual, low-key modernity

Suitably dramatic and exotic, the wrought-iron entrance gates set the aesthetic tone of the hotel

Bedrooms are bright and spacious, with walls of unrendered stone typical of this part of Turkey

The Mahzen Restaurant in the cellars is a Byzantine-inspired space moodily illuminated by jewel-like lanterns

The lobby is distinguished by a remarkable eighteenth-century Ottoman stone fireplace

In winter, breakfast is served in the library, a space straight out of an old merchant's house on the Bosphorus

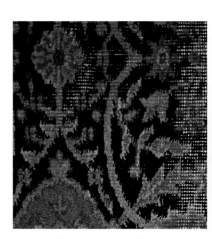

Evocative fragments of history and handcraft recall Turkey's historic role as a crossroads of civilization

Dark, cosy fireplace corners contrast with bright outdoor spaces; unlike most beach hotels, Ada is open all year round

Built in local stone and landscaped to mimic the surroundings, the hotel blends perfectly into its hillside setting

Rustic furniture, antiques and the odd splash of modernity are the signature mix of Istanbul designer Hakan Ezer

In their furniture and interior spaces, Ada's guest rooms are all completely different

Even the smallest detail, such as this water bowl in the hammam, has been carefully considered

Beautiful old kilims and prayer rugs enhance floors and walls throughout the hotel

Ada's most stunning architectural feature is its hammam, an ambitious piece of cultural authenticity

Three guest rooms are duplex suites, with a small living area downstairs and the bedroom and bathroom upstairs

From the elegant dining terrace, guests enjoy a sweeping view of Türkbükü, billed as the Turkish St Tropez

In fact, Ada blends in so well that the hotel is difficult to find, even though the town of Türkbükü is tiny. Only the domes of the hotel's captivatingly beautiful hammam identify it from a distance…and the hammam is a story in itself. This much photographed marble steam room was not only designed by an academic who wrote a thesis on the art and architecture of Turkish baths, but this PhD actually then set about building it himself, by hand.

The hammam is just one component of the historical tapestry that the owner and his designer, Istanbul-based Hakan Ezer, have managed to weave at Ada. Everywhere throughout the cleverly eclectic interiors of this fourteen-room hotel there are remnants of Turkish history that are wondrous and awe-inspiring. The lobby features a single-piece stone fireplace that even experts on Ottoman antiquity marvel at, an eighteenth-century masterpiece that has miraculously survived intact to this day. Old kilims, gelims, beautifully designed prayer mats, lamps fashioned from ox-cart wheels, portraits executed in Turkish porcelain, decorative ceiling details, old wooden *jali* screens, jugs, bowls, tiles, oil lamps: all has been taken from history and integrated tastefully into a subtle, modern, neutrally coded design scheme.

The aesthetics of this hotel are original and impressive, no question about that – but what is it like to stay there? Surprisingly, the atmosphere is even more impressive. The pieces may be priceless, but the attitude is not in the least precious. My guess is that it's the service you will remember most. There's a warm-hearted hospitality here that is not at all tainted by the attitude that sometimes accompanies such sophisticated design. And then there's the food…a gourmet reminder that Turkish cuisine is not all shish kebabs.

Turkish food, Turkish history, Turkish antiquities, Turkish modernity – Ada gives you all the Turkeys, pre- and post-independence, served on an idyllic slice of the Aegean.

---

address Ada Hotel, Göl-Türkbükü Bagarasi Mah.,Tepecik Cad. N° 128, Bodrum, 48400 Mugla, Turkey

t + 90 252 377 59 15   **f** + 90 252 377 53 79   **e** sales@adahotel.com

room rates from US$250

maçakızı

On the Turkish Riviera they do beach differently. No towels on the sand for these immaculately tanned, perfectly groomed, fashionably equipped urbanites from Istanbul. Anyway, they'll tell you, it's too hot to lie on a beach. Much better to be directly on the water, and a lot easier for swimming in the crystal-clear Aegean. So, while elsewhere in the Med the scene is *sur la plage*, in Türkbükü it's on the pontoons of the super-chic beach clubs. They have a point. There's something rather splendid about lounging around in the sun on plump Ottoman cushions surrounded on all sides by the cool waters of the Turkish Med. These wooden decks are equipped with showers, canvas-covered mattresses, overhead shades made of reeds…and that's just for the sunning–swimming area. There's also the matter of eating and drinking. The terrain behind the pontoons is carved into a series of stepped terraces that make their way up the side of the bay. The idea is you leave your towel on the pontoon and enjoy an alfresco lunch on a terrace overlooking the bathers below. Many of the beach clubs have a charcoal fire for grilling meat or fish.

They call it the Turkish Riviera, and just like St Tropez this was until not too long ago a small fishing town. Tucked into a protected bay, it's kept tolerably cool by its north-facing orientation, and during the hottest month there's almost always a sea breeze. Right now this town, a half-hour drive from Bodrum, is the favourite summer destination of the Istanbul elite. As Sahir Erozan, the proprietor of Maçakızı, explains, once upon a time people from Istanbul swam in the Bosphorus – that's why so many beautiful houses were built on or near the water. But now that the capital's population has swollen to almost fifteen million, the water has become too polluted for swimming. So people take the short flight to Bodrum and spend the season in the tiny town of Türkbükü. The scene is unbelievably *mondain*: beautifully tanned people lounging on plump canvas-covered mattresses arranged in a grid reaching into and hanging over the cool waters of the Aegean, sunning and swimming while speakers play the selection of a very hip DJ who is hidden somewhere under an olive tree. A bell rings to signal that lunch – a buffet of salads, grilled meat and seafood – is served on tables arranged on cascading terraces leading to the swimming decks.

My first encounter with the pontoon beach club experience of Türkbükü was six years ago.

Outdoor terraces carved into the rocky hillside give guests privacy while also being part of Maçakızı's scene

Pale and unadorned, Maçakızı's guest bedrooms are the deliberate opposite of the socially frenetic public spaces

The architecture of Maçakızı is a Mediterranean-modern mix of local materials and cubic forms

Most of the pristine white interiors have a view of the Aegean and the hotel's gardens; colour is all on the outside

Proprietor Sahir Erozan is a master at creating a collection of photogenic conversation spaces

Indoors, the furniture is simple and basic, just what you would expect to find in a Turkish beach house

I had never seen anything like it before, partly I guess because most governments would simply not allow structures to protrude into water that is considered public property. But in Turkey the approach is more stylishly pragmatic. Six years ago, however, Türkbükü was a day destination. There was nowhere to stay here, and so the Istanbul crowd would drive down from Bodrum for the day. The originator of the pontoon beach club concept was Sahir Erozan's mother Ayla, and his new hotel is named after her: Maçakızı, meaning Queen of Spades, is her nickname. Erozan now lives and works in Washington DC, where he is active in the restaurant business and fundraising for politics, but he spends each summer on the Bodrum peninsula. His is no longer the only pontoon beach club in Türkbükü, but the difference between Maçakızı and the rest is ambience. Night and day there is an incredibly vibrant but also relaxed atmosphere that is unashamedly hedonistic. Lunch consists of local Turkish dishes; in the evenings a more elaborate menu of Mediterranean fusion cuisine is prepared by a chef brought over from Washington. Good food, good music, great location: the formula is simple.

When Sahir Erozan first found this property it was just a big rock. Every month during the off-season he would join his workers in carving a series of terraces into the stone. The rubble they excavated was used to build the walls that define the different levels, as well as the hotel itself. Not a tree was touched in the process and numerous (mainly olives) were planted. The impression is entirely natural, even if the total expanse of the property consumes fifty tons of water a day to keep it green and lush – so lush, in fact, that apart from a couple of flags Maçakızı is almost impossible to spot from the water, despite its sixty rooms and its multi-layered terraces that can accommodate up to two hundred diners. You'd be forgiven for mistaking it for a discreet private residence – which is just the way the Turkish elite like it.

address Maçakızı Hotel, Kesireburnu Mevkii, Türkbükü, Bodrum, Mugla 48400, Turkey

t +90 252 377 6272 **f** +90 252 377 6287 **e** macakizi@superonline.com

room rates from €125

casapueblo

It may sound like pure heresy, but it is Uruguay, not Argentina, that claims credit for inventing the tango. The most famous tango tune of all, 'La Cumparsita', was composed in Montevideo by Gerardo Matos Rodriguez in 1916. It's a convincing argument, even if it is hotly disputed in Buenos Aires. But if Uruguay invented the tango, Argentina got its own back by inventing Punta del Este. This cosmopolitan, some would say flashy, beach resort might be on the Uruguayan coast, but in practice it is virtually an annex of Buenos Aires. Seen from a distance (and to be frank, Punta del Este looks better from a distance), this narrow peninsula jutting out into the azure blue Atlantic is reminiscent of Cancun: white beaches flanked by densely stacked high-rises. Up close, it is a South American cross between Miami and Ibiza. Beach bodies are bronzed, pumped and sculpted, and top international models are ubiquitous, working or not. For the duration of the summer – January, February, March – this tiny peninsula is like one big party.

But why do so many Argentinians come all the way from Buenos Aires when their own city is on the coast? The answer is simple: the Río de la Plata. This huge river estuary, with Buenos Aires on one side, Montevideo on the other, is fed by the Río Uruguay and the Río Paraná. And it is not exactly perfect bathing water. It isn't dirty, but it does look that way. All the silt churned up by the rivers' rapid flow turns the Río de la Plata into a murky brown soup. The first place where the blue waters of the Atlantic reassert themselves is some hundred miles east of Uruguay's capital, around Punta del Este.

Sparkling waters and white beaches aside, the most startling aspect of Punta is how different it is from the rest of the country. Uruguay is mostly low-key and empty. The pampas, the South American equivalent of the Outback, are home to massive cattle ranches, a gentle reminder that beef, not beach, is the real business of this nation. In the early twentieth century, Uruguay and beef were almost synonymous; towns such as Fray Bentos were to tinned beef what Hoover was to the vacuum cleaner. The statistics speak for themselves. Frigorifico Anglo del Uruguay in Fray Bentos shipped a million Oxo cubes to Europe between 1914 and 1918. Uruguay was known as the Switzerland of South America. But in time the beef trade succumbed to international competition, and the country never fulfilled its potential or achieved the financial status of its Helvetian namesake. Still, that doesn't appear to worry the average Uruguayan one little bit. This is a society where people while away the time apparently unconcerned by the latest gadget. Even the cars are very Havana. From the 1960s, '50s, '40s and even the '20s, Montevideo's *automóviles americanos* are testament to Uruguay's once-prohibitive import duties. In a word, Uruguay is old-fashioned in a Gabriel García Márquez kind of way.

Punta del Este, however, is decidedly not old-fashioned. This party place has a lot in common with St Tropez. And as any St Tropez regular will tell you, the way to survive the social frenzy of summer is to be able to retreat. And that's the magic of Casapueblo. Eight miles out of Punta, it is, architecturally speaking, in a world of its own. The whitewashed freeform organic twists, turrets and terraces that were obviously executed by hand immediately bring to mind Antonio Gaudí. Given that Gaudí was often considered more of an artist than an architect, it is fitting that this Gaudí-goes-Gaucho creation is the work of Carlos Páez

Vilaró, an acclaimed Uruguayan artist. Inspired by native farmers who build their houses in adobe, and by the moulded mud nests of the Uruguayan *hornero* or oven bird, Vilaró sought to create an architecture that would break free of the straight line. This extraordinary building was created as his atelier and a place for like-minded artists to stay and work. Its growth was organic, like the aesthetic, eventually expanding to include a museum of Vilaró's work and a seventy-room hotel with two pools, bar and restaurant. Guestrooms are freeform and cavelike with stalactite detail, and all white apart from unapologetically bright cushions and fabrics. Vilaró is inspired by *candombe*, the African-influenced dance and music of Uruguay, and it shows in the vitality of the accent colours and the overall vibe of the place.

There's a current trend for fashionable hotels to endow their spaces with works of art. At Casapueblo the formula has been turned upside down. An important work of art has been endowed with a hotel.

address   Casapueblo, Punta Ballena 20003, Uruguay

t +598 42 578041   **f** +598 42 579121   **e** reservas@clubhotel.com.ar

room rates   from US$60

the delano

When it opened in 1995 the Delano must have set a world record for the number of press inches devoted to a new hotel. Nowhere in New York, Paris or London had ever created this much of a stir. Journalists not normally easily impressed waxed lyrical about the white rooms, the white marble, the white-clad staff, the all-white spa…. The best description came from Charles Gandee, who identified the Delano as 'a safe haven for the dangerously hip', its 'blanket of white…otherworldly, dreamlike'. In short, everyone went crazy for the whiteness.

Almost a decade later, all-white rooms are no longer such a big deal. But Starck's design for the Delano's public spaces is. Not only is it, in my opinion, one of his best interiors, but it has achieved the status that all architects and designers long for: recognition as a 'classic'. With its soaring ceiling height and forest of imposing columns, it offers great visual drama. And its theatre is undiminished by the fact that it is no longer new. The Delano is Starck at his purest – pre-gimmickry. There are no gigantic Louis XVI chairs, no molar teeth turned into stools, no garden gnomes parading as tables. Instead you have a handsome Brazilian cherry floor and beautifully crafted Venetian mirrors that are imposing in their sheer size yet beautiful for their delicate detail. Then there's Starck's signature long table in alabaster marble illuminated from beneath to give it a warm glow. Even architects who regard decoration as fanciful nonsense will admit their admiration. There's also a touch of Starck as design curator in a sculptural Gaudí chair, white fibreglass Eames chairs and a series of Moor chairs created by Milanese legend Fornasetti.

The Delano is the perfect symbol of the new Miami – hip, young and design-conscious, almost European in its sophistication, definitely Latin in its love of partying and staying out late. When it opened it was one of the South Beach pioneers – not the first to recognize the potential of the neglected Art Deco towers along the beach, but certainly the first to dare *not* to be on Ocean Drive. At the time, everything from Gloria Estefan's Cuban restaurant to Gianni Versace's house and a whole slew of new-minted groovy hotels were on Ocean Drive, but the Delano – the original name of this 1947 hotel, after Franklin Delano Roosevelt – was standing all by itself in an area that was still more 'early bird' than late night.

Since then, the nonstop renovation of South Beach has attained a certain maturity. The near-hysterical hype has been replaced

with a more laid-back resignation. Even the most sceptical observers accept that with all its bars, shops, restaurants and events, Miami's South Beach is equal to New York's SoHo – except that it also has beaches and warm weather. A funny thing has also happened to the local geography. Ten years ago Ocean Drive was *the* address. South Beach *was* Ocean Drive and vice versa. The only exceptions were the Astor, a few blocks back, and the Delano, over on Collins. Despite its distinctive architecture and its direct access to the beach (unlike hotels on Ocean Drive, where you have to cross the road) the Delano was by itself. All around were boarded-up buildings, retired people in shorts, and burger joints advertising special deals for early birds. The Delano itself may have been happening, but the area decidedly was not.

Now Collins Avenue is finally poised to take the mantle from Ocean Drive, with the Sagamore and the Ritz-Carlton on one side, the Raleigh, the Townhouse and the Shore Club on the other, it offers more restaurants,

bars and nightclubs in a row than any other area of South Beach. While Ocean Drive has become a bit of a cliché, Collins still has the Latin energy that makes the city such a hot destination. And clearly, competition on every front is good for South Beach. Once upon a time, people would comment about service at the Delano: 'all the staff might look like models,' they would say, 'but they seem offended when you ask them to do something.' Now all that is history. The staff are still acceptably photogenic, but the hotel operates with all the polish and efficiency you would expect of a place that has transcended trends to establish itself as an institution. It's a powerful combination: the design, the location, the weather and the scene. For lunch, breakfast and late at night, the Delano is still a hotspot. It's fascinating to sit at reception and watch people's reaction when they first come in. Ten years on, this place has still got what it takes to make you stop and look. Messieurs Starck and Schrager: take a bow.

---

address The Delano, 1685 Collins Avenue Miami Beach, Florida 33139, USA

t +1 305 672 2000 **f** +1 305 532 0099 **e** delano@ianschragerhotels.com

room rates from US$295

the shore club

In the minimalist architectural franchise of early '90s London, John Pawson was the monk, Claudio Silvestrin the artist, and David Chipperfield the artisan. Chipperfield came to prominence in the late 1980s with his design for Equipment shirt shops. They were a revolution in retail. The concept was magnificently, almost ludicrously simple. Equipment sold silk shirts in different colours; nothing else. Chipperfield's shops were beautifully detailed boxes – immaculately thought-through containers in which nothing would interfere with the theatre of the shirts. Their success led to other high-profile commissions such as the home of photographer Nick Knight, and it was almost inevitable that Chipperfield would one day apply his practical minimalism to the design of a hotel.

So it was that in the late 1990s he began work on the Shore Club – at 325 rooms, one of the most ambitious South Beach hotel projects to date. Just one block down from the Delano, the Shore Club merged two existing beach front properties – the 1949 Shore Club and the 1939 Sharalton – with a brand new, purpose-built tower. Expectations were high. Thus far the hippification of South Beach had been largely about the renovation of existing properties. This was something different, and the Shore Club enjoyed a lot of pre-opening hype, fuelled by a tantalizing series of opening-soon teasers placed by the proprietors in all the right magazines. The Shore Club was the concrete and glass equivalent of a Hollywood blockbuster – a lot of money and reputation were riding on its eventual box office.

Chipperfield's design approach was not too dissimilar from his Equipment shops – a pared-down palette of grey terrazzo floors, white walls and white fabrics accented by the odd flash of colour. All lines were strictly architectural – pure verticals or horizontals, no curves. The only relief from the discipline came from the cone-shaped aluminium lampshades anodized in funky 1950s cocktail-shaker colours like emerald green, gold and purple. It was a bold and uncompromising scheme that united the entire hotel as one expanse. But unfortunately it flopped at the box office. Its minimal signature was popular with hard-core architects and designers; everyone else hated it. Not that the rooms were uncomfortable – quite the opposite. They were, and still are, loaded with the latest high-tech options, as well as more old-fashioned creature comforts such as plenty of closet space and enormous bathrooms.

It's just that it was all so pared-down that any chance of ambience was eliminated. Word got out that the Shore Club was 'like checking in to a hospital' or 'booking a room in an office building'.

To save a sinking ship, the proprietors called in Ian Schrager, impresario of the nearby Delano. His approach was clever and economical. He too saw there was nothing wrong with the rooms, so instead focused on the public areas. The lobby, the bars and the restaurants were all given the colour and character they had previously lacked. In some cases this meant nothing more than a curtain here, or a bold slap of Majorelle blue paint there. Other spaces like the Redroom in the Sky Bar were complete reinventions.

Three decades after Schrager and his partner Steve Rubell came to international prominence with their legendary nightclub Studio 54, Schrager has lost none of his talent for creating a buzz. In fact the Shore Club now has more buzz than any other venue in Miami.

And this time he didn't even need Philippe Starck to help him. The whole of the ground floor leading all the way to the beach has been turned into one seamless nocturnal playzone for grown-ups. Under every potted tree and around each column, there's a quirky, funky, but also cosy collection of stools, chairs, couches and tables. The lighting is low, with a few thousand candles; the music is seductively eclectic; and the design is a mix of every ethnic style that has ever contributed to the culture of chilling out – Greek taverna stools, Moroccan daybeds, Rajasthani palace chairs, Arabic tea trays, African tribal stools (in pink plastic no less), and of course cushions, cushions and more cushions in Hare Krishna colours. By coincidence I happened to be staying at the Shore Club during the full thrust of Art Basel Miami, a hugely successful Miami incarnation of the world's biggest art fair. The Shore Club was *the* after-hours party venue. The clientele were like happy little creative pigs – the Shore Club was their mud!

---

address The Shore Club, 1901 Collins Avenue, South Beach, Miami, Florida 33139, USA

t +1 305 695 3100 **f** +1 305 695 3277 **e** info@shoreclub.com

room rates from US$495

fundu lagoon

Known as the Spice Islands, the Zanzibar archipelago – including Zanzibar itself, the lesser-known Pemba and the islets of Mnemba, Tumbatu and Mafia – has long been the world's main source of cloves. However, Zanzibar's legendary wealth didn't come from the sedate business of growing spices: it came from the iniquitous profits of slavery. In the mid-nineteenth century, it was the biggest slave-trading depot on Africa's eastern coast, so lucrative that the ruling Sultan of Oman moved his official residence here. As many as 600,000 slaves are reckoned to have passed through the markets of this powerful city-state. Although the Sultanate was ousted in 1964, the country's colourful history left a cultural and architectural heritage unlike any other in East Africa. The long-standing presence of the Omani Arabs exerts a lingering influence on Zanzibar's food, clothing and of course religion, but periods of control by Portugal, Great Britain and Germany, as well as a substantial Indian population, have also left their mark. The city of Stone Town, with its exotic labyrinth of narrow streets, whitewashed coral houses, bustling bazaars and ornate mosques, is fascinating, a slightly run-down yet quixotic mix of India, Europe, Africa and Arabia.

The truth is, however, that most visitors these days do not come for the spices or the cultural legacy. They come for the beaches: the islands of Zanzibar offer some of the best diving and snorkelling in the world. The Italians in particular were quick to pick up on their potential. On Zanzibar's northeastern beaches of Nungwi and on the tiny, privately owned island of Mnemba, it was Italians who designed and built the first of a new generation of beach hotels: simple thatched huts with sand floors that pioneered the 'less is more' philosophy of desert-island lodging – Robinson Crusoe minus the hunger and the loneliness (and Man Friday).

Yet it's the neighbouring island of Pemba that offers the archipelago's most sensational diving. Unlike Zanzibar, a continental island, Pemba is an oceanic island, with a deep channel teeming with marine life. For serious divers, there are wall dives – or 'adrenalin dives' as they are known – and with Pemba's reefs offering an average underwater visibility of almost ninety feet, there is a high probability of seeing deep-sea species such as giant trevally, Napoleon wrasse, barracuda, shark and eagle ray, in between the vivid stalks and strands of hard and soft coral.

Pemba has never enjoyed the wealth or pivotal influence of its more glamorous sister island, and apart from its clove plantations, it has remained largely undeveloped. Tourism has not really got a foothold here, despite the fact that geographically speaking Pemba has more to offer than Zanzibar, as its Arabic name Al Khudra or 'Green Island' suggests: where Zanzibar is flat and sandy, Pemba is hilly and densely vegetated. So though few travellers make the effort to go to Pemba, those who do are richly rewarded.

One such visitor was British fashion designer Ellis Flyte, who was so struck by the island's hidden beauty that she returned to create this idyllic retreat. The spot she chose (or she might say chose her) was not, and still is not, accessible by road. To this day, the only way to get to Fundu Lagoon is by private boat, and even then, blink and you'll miss it. If it weren't for the bar that sits at the end of the handcrafted jetty, I doubt anyone would ever find it.

Fundu's guests are accommodated in Peter Beard-style designer tents set under traditional thatched roofs on top of wooden platforms on stilts. The owners describe the place as a barefoot paradise, and for once it's true: Fundu Lagoon could double as a set for a Robinson Crusoe film tomorrow. There are no shops or hotels in the vicinity. As a guest you have little choice but to unwind and go native (although in the presence of locals you had better keep at least some of your clothes on, since devout Muslims are offended by nudity).

This rustic, back-to-nature, thatched-hut approach is not unique. There are more than a handful of places around the globe that subscribe to it. What gives Fundu the edge are its fashion connection and its world-class diving, complete with a fully-fledged diving school that caters to all levels. At Fundu you get two paradises: one above the water and one below. Here, you can be Crusoe and Cousteau in the same day.

---

address Fundu Lagoon, Pemba, Zanzibar, Tanzania

t +255 74 74 38 688 **f** +255 24 22 32 926 **e** fundu@africaonline.co.tz

room rates from US$240

HIP™
HOTELS

First published in 2004 in paperback in the United States of America by Thames & Hudson Inc., 500 Fifth Avenue, New York, New York 10110

thamesandhudsonusa.com

Library of Congress Catalog Card Number 2003112786
ISBN 0-500-28486-5

Printed and bound in Singapore by CS Graphics

Acknowledgments

Photography by Herbert Ypma, with the exception of the Chedi, North Island, Birkenhead House, Casapueblo and Fundu Lagoon, supplied courtesy of the hotels.

Designed by Maggi Smith